THE BRITISH ANTI-SLAVERY
MOVEMENT

THE
HOME UNIVERSITY LIBRARY
OF MODERN KNOWLEDGE

For list of volumes in the Library see end of book.

THE BRITISH ANTI-SLAVERY MOVEMENT

By

R. COUPLAND
C.I.E., M.A.

BEIT PROFESSOR OF COLONIAL HISTORY
IN THE UNIVERSITY OF OXFORD

1933.

LONDON:
THORNTON BUTTERWORTH, LIMITED

First Published *1933*

CONTENTS

PREFACE

THE material incorporated in this book was used for a course of lectures delivered at the Lowell Institute at Boston in March, 1933.

The author has been greatly assisted, especially in Chapters V and VI, by the works of Dr. W. L. Mathieson, and he is further indebted to him for reading and criticizing those chapters in proof. Parts of the book have also been kindly read in proof by Mr. R. Pares, and the last chapter by Sir John Harris.

R. C.

WOOTTON HILL,
May, 1933.

CHAPTER I

THE AFRICAN SLAVE-SYSTEM

A Slave, said Aristotle, is "a living tool," and Slavery may be defined as the ownership and use of human property. The master inherits, buys, sells or bequeaths his slave as he does his pick or his spade. His treatment of him or her may be controlled, like the usage of other possessions, by the custom or law of the society to which he belongs ; but in general the slave's life and labour are as much at the master's disposal as those of his horse or his ass. As with a beast of burden, the slave's health and happiness depend on chance—on the character of his master and on the nature of his work. He may be well cared for ; he may even sometimes seem better off than if he had never been enslaved ; or he may be cruelly treated, underfed, overworked, done to death. But Slavery stands condemned more on moral than on material grounds. It displays in their extreme form the evils which attend the subjection of the weak to the strong. The slave's soul is almost as much in bondage as his body. His choice of conduct is narrowly prescribed. He cannot lead his own life. He can do little to make or mar his fate : it lies in another man's hands. Though Slavery was regarded by the founders of Western civilization as a natural and permanent element in human society, it was recognized that enslavement inflicted a moral injury. " Zeus takes away the half of a man's virtue," sang Homer, " when the day of slavery comes upon him." It was not so widely understood that Slavery might be injurious to the masters' morals also.

From the beginning of history Slavery has been practised among men. It was a universal element in the social and economic structure of all ancient civilization—in that of China, India, Persia, Mesopotamia, Egypt, Greece and Rome. And, though its character varied at different times and places, it had certain more or less common features. The slaves were usually obtained in two ways, which might be termed " internal " and " external." Within a society, a man might be enslaved as a punishment for crime or might sell himself or his children into slavery to pay a debt. From outside the society, slaves were acquired by the capture of enemies in war. This happened sometimes on a great scale. Whole tribes or communities might be carried off from their homeland, like the people of Judaea to Babylon. At an early date, also —it is impossible to say how early—a trade in slaves developed. Traders kidnapped and purchased slaves from primitive or defenceless peoples and sold them in the markets of the civilized world. The use of the slaves acquired in these ways was broadly of two kinds. Domestic Slavery, which may be taken to cover the employment of slaves in gardens or small farms or shops as well as in the house or the harem, was the universal type, and it was or might be relatively mild. The domestic slave could achieve a personal relationship with his master. He could develop an individuality of his own. He might even become in some sort a member of the family. None of this was possible in the other and less general kind of Slavery—the employment of slaves in gangs for large-scale industry or agriculture. It was this mass-use of human labour that required the sternest discipline and involved the greatest cruelty; and no sentimental apologies for slavery can mitigate the tragedy of the nameless thousands who built the pyramids of Egypt and the palaces of Nineveh and Babylon or worked the silver-mines of Attica or tilled the Roman *latifundia*.

With the advance of civilization Slavery slowly declined. In Europe the cessation of Roman conquest diminished the supply of slaves, and the spread of Christianity, though it countenanced their ownership, tended to improve their treatment and raise their status. Gang-slavery for public works or on big agricultural estates disappeared. Domestic Slavery was gradually transformed into the looser bondage of serfdom or villeinage, and so proceeded, more

9

slowly in backward Eastern Europe than in the
progressive Western countries, towards complete
emancipation. In Asia, likewise, the range and
volume of enslavement were contracted. Wars
and conquests continued : there was no " Roman
peace " ; but from the eighth century onwards the chief conquering races, Turk or
Arab, were Moslems whose main incentive was
to force the peoples they conquered to embrace
their creed ; and the Koran, while, like the
Bible, it accepted the institution of Slavery,
declared that no Moslem might be enslaved.
Thus, throughout the great belt of Moslem Asia
which stretched across the " Middle East "—
the Turkish Empire, Arabia, Persia, Northern
India—Slavery would presumably have died
a natural death, more quickly perhaps than in
Europe, if it had not been possible for those
countries to obtain a steady supply of slaves
from unconquered lands and by other means
than conquest. Such a supply, as it happened,
was available in one vast area of the Old World,
beyond the reach of Moslem armies but not of
Moslem slave-traders. Asia's need was met by
Africa.

The records of human history had so far been
concerned with the white and brown and yellow
races only. The black race—the Negroes and
kindred negroid stock—had lived an isolated life
in their mid-African homeland between the
Sahara and the Zambesi, unknowing and almost
unknown to the rest of mankind. A huge

natural barrier of desert and swamp secluded them from the stream of civilization, European or Asiatic, flowing through the Mediterranean and the Near East. Their tropical environment had made it easy for them to live, but difficult to do much more. Their country contained no great navigable rivers or alluvial plains such as facilitated the growth of an indigenous civilization in Egypt, Mesopotamia, Northern India or China. Leagues of forest or jungle, chains of mountains, parching drought and swamping rains confined their movements and restricted intercourse. Here and there a vigorous tribe attained a substantial measure of military and even political organization ; but there was nothing remotely comparable with the social or cultural achievements of Europe and Asia ; and the great mass of the Africans—for these black people of the Tropics and not the mixed Berber and Semitic races of the northern coastland are the true Africans—stayed sunk in primitive barbarism, the most backward of all the major races of men. To more fortunate and forward folk in other continents they seemed at first contact to be little above the animals ; and centuries were to pass before they were allowed the opportunity of proving their capacity to take their place in the march of human progress. But in one thing, it seemed from the outset, they excelled—in physical strength. They could work, or be made to work with a whip, both hard and long. If slaves were needed, therefore, they

11

provided the ideal material. As the Greeks would have put it, they were φύσει δούλοι, " slaves by nature " ; and even to Christians of a later day they seemed almost to have been created for the purpose. What else could be the meaning of the curse of Ham ?

It was easy enough, moreover, for the agents of the outer world to get slaves from among them, once they had found the way to their homes. Enslavement was no new thing in Central Africa. It had never, indeed, been practised there on such a scale as in Egypt or Asia. Gang-slavery belongs to a far higher civilization than the Africans had attained, and there is nothing to suggest their use of it except the great ruins of mysterious Zimbabwe and its fellow-sites in Rhodesia. But domestic Slavery seems to have been a normal feature of African life. A conquering tribe would enslave the women and children of the conquered tribe and sometimes, if it spared their lives, the men. It was not difficult, therefore, for the alien trader to tempt a chief with strange and desirable goods from afar—in later days the most irresistible commodities were firearms and alcohol—to sell some of the slaves in his village or, better still, to attack a neighbouring village and sell such of its inhabitants as could be caught. And the trader himself, if he had a well-armed following and was operating among unwarlike tribes, might effect a raid on his own account.

In course of time African slaves were exported

from the whole of the midland zone, from the
foothills of Abyssinia to the coast of the Gulf
of Guinea and Angola ; but the main source of
supply was always in the very heart of the continent—the equatorial area between the Upper
Nile, the Upper Congo and the Great Lakes,
where, broadly speaking, the teeming population
was least civilized, least organized, and most
defenceless. From this inexhaustible reservoir
the stream of Negro slaves began to flow northwards as soon as contact was established by way
of the Nile between the southern Sudan and
Egypt or by the caravan-routes across the
Sahara between the Niger and Congo country
and the Greek, Phœnician and Roman cities on
the Mediterranean coast. A third line of export
ran eastwards to the shore of the Indian Ocean
where, long before the rise of Islam, Arab colonists from Oman had begun to found a string of
trading-towns all down the coast from Somaliland to the Zambesi.

When the great wave of Arab conquest, im-
pelled by Islam, ran right along the north coast
of Africa to the Atlantic, those three threads of
the Slave Trade were all in Arab hands, and
from the ninth century it was mainly Arab
traders who supplied the demand of the Moslem
world for slaves. Nor was it only in the markets
of the Arab or, later on, the Turkish Empire—
at Fez, Tunis, Cairo, Damascus, Mecca, Bagdad
—that they sold their human wares. From the
East African ports, especially Kilwa, a steady

stream of slaves was carried across the Indian Ocean to the Persian Gulf and thence inland to Persia or along the coast to India. As late as the fifteenth century there were thousands of African slaves in the Moslem kingdom of Bengal. And in the great days of Arab history (c. A.D. 900–1300) when Arab ships were masters of the Eastern seas and Arab trading-posts were dotting all their coasts, the unhappy Africans were borne still farther from their homes. In A.D. 976 a sensation was caused at the court of the Emperor of China by the arrival of an Arab envoy with a " Negro slave " in his suite.

Thus, year after year and century after century, the depopulation of Africa by Asia went on. The average annual number of slaves exported may not have been great—not more, perhaps, than a few thousands ; but since the process continued without a break till the end of the nineteenth century, the total volume of this Asiatic branch of the Slave Trade must have been enormous. And that was not all that Africa had to suffer. Another vast multitude of Africans were stolen away from their homeland when Europe joined Asia in the game.

Of the European peoples it was the Portuguese who began it, for the simple reason that they were the first to make close contact with mid-Africa. The existence of a rich fertile country to the south of the bare Atlantic seaboard of Morocco had been made known to

Europe from the works of Arab geographers, and
at the outset of the fifteenth century, the Portuguese, following up and going beyond the earlier
Genoese ventures, pushed on, bit by bit, down
the African coast till in 1445 they reached the
Senegal. This southward track was to lead
them farther than they had dreamed—round the
Cape of Good Hope to India and to the naval
and commercial mastery of the East. But those
first voyages down the African coast were
organized by Dom Henrique, popularly known
as " Henry the Navigator," son of King João I
and nephew through his Lancastrian mother of
Henry IV of England, with the limited idea of
founding a Portuguese dominion on the Gulf of
Guinea, pushing east to link up with the Christians of Abyssinia, and so taking the " Moors "
of North Africa in the rear : and, ironically
enough, it was to finance this " last crusade "
against the Moslems that Christian Europe first
took part in the African Slave Trade. Dom
Henrique instructed his adventurers to try to
tap the traffic at its source in Guinea and to
bring by sea to Portugal those valuable Negroes
whom the Arabs had long brought across the
desert to Tunis and Morocco : and in 1441 two
of his captains secured twelve men, women and
children from the neighbourhood of the Rio
d'Ouro and presented them to their delighted
master. The business thus begun grew swiftly.
Licences to pursue it were freely given by Dom
Henrique. In 1444 six caravels set out from

Lagos on a " joint-stock " enterprise, and came back laden with 235 slaves. By 1448, when the Senegal and the Gambia had been reached and passed, a total of nearly 1,000 slaves had been imported : and as the explorers sailed farther and farther south, to the Congo and Angola and finally round the Cape to Mozambique, the imports rose with the expansion of the sources of supply.

So Slavery, which had long died out in Western Europe, was re-established on its soil. Most of the slaves were sold to Portuguese landowners who used them to cultivate the areas laid waste in the recent Moorish wars. The results, social as well as economic, were bad ; and it seems improbable that the experiment would in any case have been long sustained. As it was, the import of slaves dwindled and ceased as soon as it was discovered that gold and ivory were more profitable articles of export from West Africa ; and, though it is said that several thousand Negroes were being sold every year in the slave-market at Lisbon as late as 1539, by that time the untold wealth of India and the Far East had been opened up, and thenceforward Portuguese traders were unlikely to waste ships in fetching slaves. But the European Slave Trade was not destined to be a relatively mild and transient infliction upon Africa. The age of exploration had opened the West as well as the South and East—the West Indies and America as well as West Africa and the Indian Ocean.

Colonization had followed on exploration. And just when Europeans in the Old World had realized that they had no real need for Negroes, Europeans in the New World discovered that they could not do without them.

In the half-century after Columbus first landed in the Bahamas in 1492 the Spaniards conquered and partly occupied a huge area stretching from Mexico through Peru to Uruguay and including all the larger West Indian islands, while in 1531 the Portuguese began the colonization of Brazil. At once the newcomers set themselves to exploit the great natural wealth of their acquisitions, to work the gold and silver mines on the mainland and to lay out plantations of tobacco, indigo and sugar in the rich soil of the islands and Brazil. But they were soon confronted by the difficulty of procuring the requisite supply of labour. A great deal of it was needed, and the cost of white men's wages and the heat of the tropical sun made it virtually impossible for the Europeans to provide it themselves. Of the native Indians many had been massacred during the conquest, many had fled to the mountains and forests, and even where sufficient numbers were available it was soon apparent that they did not possess the stamina required for continuous and exacting toil. This labour-difficulty would in fact have indefinitely retarded the economic development of most of the New World if the Portuguese had not recently shown how it could be overcome. Christians in the West could do what Moslems in the East had done. America was saved by Africa.

The first batch of slaves from Guinea arrived in Haiti in 1510, and in Cuba in 1521. By another stroke of irony their import into the mainland Spanish colonies was stimulated by the humanitarian zeal of the Spanish missionaries. In 1514, the benevolent Las Casas, first Bishop of Mexico, began to denounce the cruelties inflicted on the Indians and to plead—how unwisely he realized too late—that Indian slaves should be replaced by African. So Africans were shipped across the Atlantic in fast-increasing numbers : by 1576 there were some 40,000 of them in Spanish America. Meantime the Portuguese had adopted the same expedient and begun to shift the people of their colony in Angola across the narrows of the South Atlantic to their colony in Brazil. Already in 1585 there were 10,000 Negroes in the single province of Pernambuco. Since, moreover, the Portuguese alone controlled the area of export in West Africa, the supply of slaves to the Spanish colonies was mainly in their hands, and after 1580 it was wholly entrusted to them by the Spanish Government under an agreement known as the *Asiento*. It was a paying business. Indeed, the economic life of Portugal in the sixteenth and seventeenth centuries was largely grounded on the profits of the Slave Trade.

Neither tropical colonization nor the control of the slave-supply, by which alone, it seemed, such colonies could be effectively exploited, remained for long the exclusive privilege of the Iberian peoples. From the end of the sixteenth century onwards the other sea-going nations of Europe—the Dutch, the French, the English— began to encroach on Spanish and Portuguese preserves. At the outset of the eighteenth century the Dutch, for example, possessed the East Indies, Ceylon, the Cape, and Surinam (Guiana); the French Île de France (Mauritius), Louisiana, the western part of Haiti, Guadeloupe and other West Indian islands; and the English the Bahamas, Jamaica and other islands, and Honduras. And, like the Spanish and Portuguese before them, Dutch, French and English began from the beginning of their occupation to stock these colonies with slaves. Nor did they leave the supply of them to the Portuguese. They intruded into the Gulf of Guinea, established fortified posts on its coast, and took their own share in the Slave Trade. Even Denmark secured a foothold there to supply the Spanish colonies by way of St. Thomas and St. Croix. So the outward flow of Africans was immensely increased. A minor part of it went eastwards; for a short time to the East Indies, continuously to Île de France and its satellites. Another small part halted midway at the Cape; most of the 1,700 slaves in the Colony in 1708 came from West or East Africa or Madagascar. But far the most of it streamed over the Atlantic and went on streaming year after year, right through the eighteenth century. Some rough figures may suggest its volume. About 1800 there were 776,000 Negroes in Spanish America. Between 1759 and 1803 from S. Paolo de Loanda and Benguela, the ports of Angola, 642,000 slaves were shipped to Brazil. About 1775 the slaves in the French West Indies numbered over 500,000. These high numbers were mainly due to the extensive and continually extending cultivation of sugar. Jamaica, the greatest British " sugar-island," contained 140,000 Negroes in 1764 and 300,000 in 1800. Nor had Slavery been confined to the zone of the Caribbean : it had spread to North America. In 1620, when the colony of Virginia was fourteen years old, the first slaves, a batch of twenty, were landed at Jamestown from a Dutch ship. By 1760 those twenty had grown to 200,000, about half the total population. In the thirteen English colonies which were presently to constitute the United States, the blacks in 1760 were 30 per cent of the whites. North of Maryland, where they numbered 8 per cent, they were only employed as domestic or farm slaves : in the South they were mainly used in gangs for cultivating sugar and tobacco and, later, cotton. Thus in the southern part of North America as well as in the West Indies and South America it was the worse kind of Slavery which Europe had revived—gang-slavery—a kind which demanded vast numbers of slaves, which precluded their natural increase, and which therefore required for its maintenance an increasing inflow of fresh stock. The total volume of this inflow was so huge as to startle the imagination. When the trans-Atlantic Slave Trade was at its height in the second half of the eighteenth century, it is certain that in one or two single years the number of slaves transported exceeded 100,000. An authoritative calculation made more than a century ago fixed the total of slaves imported into the English colonies in America and the West Indies between 1680 and 1786 at 2,130,000. Guesses at the total for all the European colonies have gone as high as 40,000,000. But, if half or less than half that figure be accepted, and if it be remembered that the European Slave Trade was to continue in full volume till past the middle of the nineteenth century, that an incalculable multitude must be added for the Arab Slave Trade, that it was the young and virile Africans who were taken and the old and feeble who were left, and finally that (as will presently be explained) in the process of obtaining one seasoned African slave the life of at least one other African was lost, then there is nothing surprising in the fact that the population of modern Africa is relatively small.

In this business of depopulating Africa the English took a large share. One of the first Englishmen known to have had a hand in it was the Elizabethan seaman, Sir John Hawkins, who, violating the Portuguese monopoly, made several voyages to West Africa between 1562 and 1567 and sold the slaves he obtained in the Spanish colonies. But the earlier chartered-companies formed for the African trade dealt mainly in gold, and it was not till 1663 that a regular English Slave Trade began with the grant of the monopoly thereof to " The Company of Royal Adventurers of England trading with Africa." Once started, it rapidly increased. In 1697, when the monopoly was abolished, about 5,000 slaves a year were being carried in English ships, and, when at the Peace of Utrecht in 1713 England obtained the coveted *Asiento*, she soon took the lead of all the other sea-powers. By 1770 about half the total Trade was carried by 192 British slave-ships with cargo-space for nearly 50,000 slaves ; and, though the British figure dropped after the loss of the American Colonies, in 1787 it still stood first at 38,000. The French came second, ranging from 20,000 to 30,000 ; the Portuguese third, with about 10,000. Of the British portion of the Trade Liverpool secured more than half by 1770 and as much as six-sevenths by the end of the century. London and Bristol shared most of what Liverpool left.

Though doubtless some slave-traders were more brutal than others, the methods of the Trade as practised by all the maritime nations of Europe were much the same. In the early days slaves could be rounded up by sudden landings on the coast ; but in time the natives learned to watch for the coming of the ships and take refuge in the bush; and, though adventurous traders sometimes penetrated inland themselves, their usual custom was to do business with professional native or half-caste dealers who took the cheap goods they had brought from Europe—cloth, beads, hardware, muskets and powder, spirit—and bartered them for slaves with chiefs up-country. There is nothing to show that the chiefs, of the stronger tribes at any rate, resisted or wanted to resist the fascination of these wares, especially the guns and drink. Enslavement within a tribe, it was observed, became the penalty for less and less serious offences; and intertribal warfare with slaves for its motive as well as the kidnapping of women and children in peace-time became a more or less constant feature of African life, spreading steadily into the interior of the continent with the steady infiltration of the Trade. Having bought his slaves, the dealer marshalled them, men, women, and children, in a caravan for the march, sometimes a very long march, to the coast. They were usually fettered to prevent escape and often locked in the "slave-stick"—a long pole with a crutch at the end for fastening round the neck. They carried on their heads the loads of foodstuffs and other baggage required for the journey or the ivory or other native produce which the dealer might have bought. The rigours of the march were often too much for the weaker members of the party. Slaves who fell sick were killed or left to die. The more frequented slave-tracks were strewn with human bones.

Arrived at the coast, they were stowed on board the slave-ships which were specially fitted for their reception. The hold was divided horizontally by decks about three feet apart with a gangway down the middle. On these shelves the slaves were laid, handcuffed in pairs, men and women in separate holds. Since the bigger the cargo, the bigger the profit, they were sometimes packed so tightly that they could scarcely turn round. A ship of 150 tons could be made to carry as many as 600 slaves. The direct voyage to Brazil was fairly short, but the so-called " Middle Passage " to the West Indies —the main centre of distribution—might be protracted for several weeks by adverse or dropping winds. If it was calm enough, the slaves were brought up on deck and urged or forced to dance for exercise. In rough weather the condition of the hold may be imagined. Disease, of course, was rife on board. Though instruments were provided for forcibly feeding those who refused to eat, it was reckoned in the later eighteenth century that on the average at least one-sixth of a cargo died on the voyage. For the ships' captains and their European crews, also, the conditions were almost as dangerous as they were brutalizing : the death-rate on slave-ships was far higher than in any other branch of the merchant-service. It was not for nothing that the malarious African coast

earned its title of " The White Man's Grave,"
and among the ditties sung by British seamen
on all the seven seas was

> Beware and take care of the Bight of Benin
> There's one comes out for forty go in.

As the end of the voyage approached, the slaves
were examined and prepared for sale. Wounds,
caused by storm or ill-usage, were doctored up
and, as far as possible, concealed. But the
agents at the ports often complained that the
" parcels of negroes " landed were " bad " or
" mean " or " much abused." Finally, on ship-
board or in the public slave-market, the slaves
were put up for sale by " scramble " or auction.
The price of a healthy man rose as high as £60
during the eighteenth century. The sick and
injured were lumped with feeble women and
children and sold off cheap as " refuse." Even
when at last they reached the plantations, the
slaves had to face one more ordeal before they
settled down to endure what was left to them
of life. The first few months of employment
were known as the period of " seasoning," and
during it no less on an average than one-third
of the novices failed to adjust themselves in
body or spirit to the new conditions of climate
or food or labour and died. Taking all the
deaths together—in the slave-catching wars or
raids, on the march to the sea, during the
" Middle Passage " and in " seasoning "—it has
been moderately reckoned that for every African

who became a " seasoned " slave at least one other African was killed.

The conditions of Slavery were least oppressive in the Spanish colonies except in the earliest and latest phases of their history. Throughout the long middle period the Crown and the Church combined to alleviate the slaves' lot. Masters were required to prepare their slaves for baptism, to ensure their attendance at Mass, and to provide facilities for marriage. If slaves on separate estates desired to marry, the master of one was compelled to buy the other at a valuation. No marriage could be broken up by the sale of either party. The freeing of slaves by their masters was encouraged as a virtue, and the slaves, who by custom, though not in law, were able to acquire property, could purchase their manumission at a fair price. An ill-treated slave could apply to the local magistrate, whose duty it was as " Protector of the Slaves " to assist in all such matters, for a licence to be sold, and such a sale became compulsory if a purchaser could be found who was willing to liberate the slave after a reasonable time or at a low price. It is not surprising, therefore, to find that by the end of the eighteenth century the number of free Negroes in some Spanish colonies was at least two-thirds of the number of slaves.

Though the Government of France was also an absolute monarchy and its Church Roman Catholic, French Slavery was far less humane than Spanish. Regulations, such as Louis XIV's *Code Noir*, were made but not enforced : and in French Haiti (St. Domingue), at any rate, the treatment of the slaves was at least as bad as in any other colony.

Nor could British Slavery bear comparison with Spanish. Though the Imperial Parliament never waived, and in the end was forced to use, its supreme legislative authority to deal with Slavery, the regulation of it was normally regarded as a domestic matter to be settled by the local legislatures in those colonies which possessed representative government, and more or less in deference to local opinion in those " Crown Colonies " where legislation was under official control. That meant as a rule that the slaves were treated as their masters and their white dependants wished ; and that in turn, for a complex of reasons, meant a *régime* of repression. Surrounded by an overwhelming multitude of barbarous Negroes, most owners were convinced that a policy of "amelioration" which aimed, not merely at protecting them from excessive cruelty, but at educating and civilizing them, was doubly bound to lead to trouble. On the one hand, the slaves would acquire new ideas, a new sense of their rights and of their power to obtain them—a process which would excite their discontent, impair their willingness to work, and culminate in a general and irresistible rebellion : on the other hand, their rise in the scale of civilization would make it increasingly difficult and finally impossible to justify the institution of Slavery itself. As it was, in their primitive state, they could be and commonly were regarded as virtually disqualified by nature for the enjoyment of human rights. Edward Long, an official in Jamaica, whose well-known history of the island was published in 1774, desired that slaves should be humanely treated, but he argued at some length that they should be classed with orang-outangs as " a different species of the same genus." To keep them thus like " living tools " or domestic animals, with no hope of ever climbing the partition which shut them off from civilized human life—such was the basic idea which, broadly speaking, inspired the owners' attitude. Manumission was always disliked and discouraged, and, though as in the Spanish colonies, the acquisition of property was permitted by usage to British slaves and they could usually sell the surplus produce of the plots of ground allotted them for growing their own food, the buying of their freedom was often obstructed by the exaction of a price far higher than the market-rate. Thus in 1827 Spanish Cuba alone contained many more free Negroes than the whole of the British islands. Christian propaganda was similarly discouraged. Though the law in early times required that slaves should be prepared for baptism, it was illegal in the southern American colonies to teach them to read; and in the West Indies, when the great missionary movement at the end of the eighteenth century at last inspired a serious effort to convert the slaves, the missionaries were usually opposed and sometimes persecuted by the white community because they fostered in slaves' minds the dangerous idea of rights. Naturally, therefore, marriages between slaves were rare. They were allowed no legal validity and could be broken by sale. In most of the islands they never occurred. But the most striking and injurious feature of the system of repression was the fact that a slave was debarred, except in a court martial, from giving evidence against anyone who was not a slave. This meant that such "ameliorating" laws as were passed from time to time could rarely be enforced. A white man could only be convicted of cruelty, however gross, or even murder if the circumstantial evidence was sufficient or if someone who was not a slave had witnessed it. A Chief Justice of St. Vincent's, himself a planter, once admitted that owing to this rule of evidence "White men are in a manner put beyond the reach of the law."

Shocking brutalities were committed under cover of this impunity. If the ways of the slaves were often provocative, especially their addiction to petty theft, the punishments inflicted on them by their irritated masters were no less often barbarous. Flogging, sometimes protracted and repeated, was the most common form, and visitors to the West Indies were frequently shocked by the scars they observed on slaves' bodies, male and female. Other forms are described in the following letter from a resident in Antigua in 1787 :

The punishments inflicted on slaves in this island, are various and tormenting . . . among which is the thumbscrew, a barbarous invention to fasten the thumbs together, which appears to cause excruciating pain. The " iron necklace " is a ring, locked or rivetted about the neck ; to these collars are frequently added . . . which prevent the wearers from laying down their heads with any degree of comfort. The " boots " are strong iron rings, full four inches in circumference, closed just above the ankles ; to these some owners prefix a chain, which the miserable sufferers, if able to work, must manage as well as they can, and it is not unfrequent to see in the streets of this town, at midday, negroes chained together by these necklaces as well as the boots. . . . The " spurs " are rings of iron, similar to the boots, to which are added spikes from three to four inches long, placed horizontally. A chain fastened about the body with a padlock, is another mode of tormenting this oppressed race of beings. A boy who has not yet seen his fourteenth year passes by my house several times in a day and has done so for these six months past with no other clothing. . . .

This is grim reading, and those who desire still more painful evidence will find as much as they can stomach in official records and the literature of the anti-Slavery movement. But the men who hated Slavery most and fought it hardest never made the mistake of judging a whole class by the vices of individuals. " I sincerely believe," wrote Wilberforce in 1823, " many of the owners of West Indian estates to be men of more than common kindness and liberality." Often, indeed, the attitude of slaves to their masters was by no means unfriendly ; and if proof were needed that the cruelties of the slave-system were not generally unendurable, it might be found in the fact that the slaves rarely rebelled and that even in the course of rebellions they rarely murdered white men.

None the less, the system was a cruel system, for it rested on an economic basis which made it almost inevitable that its human tools should be inhumanely used. The worst enemy of the slaves, it has been truly said, was sugar. For, in the first place, the cultivation of sugar necessitated gang-slavery instead of the usually milder *régime* of the small farm. Secondly, sugar, as cultivated in the eighteenth century, set a greater strain on the slaves' physique, especially at crop-time, than any other product. Thirdly, the character of the sugar-trade led to this strain being maintained at the utmost practicable pressure. It was a highly speculative business. Failures and forced sales were more usual than successes in the " West Indian lottery." Estates were always changing hands. And the upshot was that the type of true " colonist "—who had made his family home in the island, who took a patriotic interest in its general welfare, whose plantations

31

were handed on from father to son, intact and with their slaves unsold, so that the slaves tended to become attached to the estate and to merge into serfs—this old colonial type grew rarer, especially in Jamaica, and its place was taken by owners who regarded ownership as a livelihood rather than a life, a gamble rather than a responsibility. Many such owners remained in England and ran their plantations through paid managers; and most of those who went out had no other ambition than to get rich quickly and come home again. Thus the production of sugar was carried on in a tense unhealthy atmosphere in which the better elements in human nature tended to be thrust aside by the hard exigencies of getting the maximum results in the minimum time. All owners were not so callous as those who said it paid them best to work their slaves to death and buy new ones, nor was every slave-gang whipped to its work. The following description, for example, from a plantation in Dominica in 1791 suggests a happy party of free labourers such as every visitor to present-day Africa has seen and heard.

It is pleasing to see them at work, they being all together in one row, like a regiment of soldiers, and all their hoes moving together; the women singing some ludicrous songs of their own composing, which are answered in the same manner by the men, and each striving to outdo the other.

But of the " driving system," on some estates

32

at any rate, a truer version is the following, again from the eyewitness in Antigua.

The negroes are turned out at sunrise, and employed in gangs from twenty to sixty, or upwards, under the inspection of white overseers, generally poor Scotch lads, who, by their assiduity and industry, frequently become masters of the plantations, to which they came out as indentured servants. Subordinate to these overseers are drivers, who are mostly black or mulatto fellows of the worst dispositions ; these men are furnished with whips, which, while on duty, they are obliged on pain of severe punishment to have with them, and are authorized to flog wherever they see the least relaxation from labour ; nor is it a consideration with them, whether it proceeds from idleness or inability, paying, at the same time, little or no regard to age or sex. At twelve they are turned in (that is, leave off work) to get what they can to refresh nature with ; at half-past one the bell rings, when they turn out and resume their labour until sunset. . . .

No doubt conditions varied from island to island and from plantation to plantation ; but the hard fact remains that, except on the best-managed plantations, the death-rate was abnormally high. And to that fact and to the low fertility of the slave-population—caused by the unnatural conditions of its life, the disproportionate number of males, the absence of civilizing influences, the discouragement of marriage and the prevalence of promiscuous intercourse—was due the con-

B

tinuance of the Slave Trade with its worse cruelties. There were roughly 40,000 slaves in Jamaica in 1690 and 340,000 in 1820, and between those dates about 800,000 were imported.

Nor, of course, were the evil effects of the slave-system limited to the Negroes. The moral strain involved in the absolute ownership of other human beings is more than an average man can bear, and in the old West Indies it was accentuated by the economic conditions of the white men's business, by their isolation from their home-country and its sanctions, and by the risks and temptations of the climate. The old " colonial " families were in some respects a real aristocracy, but many of the fortune-hunters who supplanted them on their estates were of another character—irresponsible, arrogant, bigoted, drinking hard and gambling high, cohabiting with slave-women as a matter of course, and commonly short-lived. The most feckless of them sank to be " poor whites "— that pitiable class of white men whose social and moral state is as low as that of black men and often lower, the existence of which was the inevitable concomitant of Slavery and which still indeed exists in those " mixed " or bi-racial societies of to-day, as in the Southern States, or South Africa, which have abandoned Slavery but still recruit their main labour-force from the backward race alone.

The defenders of the slave-system ignored or denied its degrading influence on their own race.

They even argued that Slavery benefited its black victims by saving them from primitive barbarism and bringing them into contact with a higher civilization. But such an excuse, which at the best could scarcely apply to more than a favoured minority of slaves, was no real palliation of the moral injustice and inherent cruelty of Slavery, and for the sheer bestiality of the Slave Trade there could be no excuse at all. Yet Slavery and the Slave Trade were not only tolerated but more or less actively supported by public opinion in all the maritime states of Western Europe for three or four hundred years and were only abandoned at last in the course of the nineteenth century. That is a startling comment on the process of civilization. If in other fields of human relationship the world was moving forward, in that field it was going back, restoring to a new and unnatural life the dead wrongs of the past ; and, though historians must hesitate to judge their ancestors by the standards of their own day, it is difficult not to regard this treatment of Africa by Christian Europe, following Moslem Asia, as the greatest crime in history.

slave population g w.I.
700.000 to 1500.000 from 1790 to 1820.
Cotton slaves' work not s. severe as
an Sugar plantations.

CHAPTER II

THE ABOLITION OF SLAVERY IN THE BRITISH ISLES

"THAT such a system," said Wilberforce, "should so long have been suffered to exist in any part of the British Empire will appear to our posterity almost incredible." But it must be remembered that modern humanitarianism was only just coming to birth in Wilberforce's time. The treatment of children and animals, the provision for the destitute, the sick, the insane, the punishment of crime—in all such matters the standards of the eighteenth century were far below those of to-day. It must be remembered, too, that the inhumanities of the slave-system lay beyond the range of the ordinary, unimaginative, stay-at-home Englishman's personal experience. He did not see the slave-ships on the "Middle Passage," nor hear the cracking of the whips which called the slaves to work on the plantations. And, of course, there were other more positive and concrete reasons for the long continuance of Slavery and the Slave Trade.

(1) There was, first, the economic argument —that the produce of the slave-using colonies was an indispensable element in the commercial

system on which the Old Empire was based, that it could only be grown by slave-labour, and that since, on the one hand, the number of slaves in use at any time could not seemingly be increased or even maintained by breeding and since, on the other hand, new plantations were being constantly developed and new islands occasionally acquired by conquest, only by means of the Trade could the requisite number of slaves be supplied. A pamphlet, printed in London in 1709, was significantly entitled *The African Slave Trade the great Pillar and Support of the British Plantations in America*; and fifty-five years later another pamphlet declared that the Slave Trade had only one excuse, economic " necessity." " The impossibility of doing without slaves in the West Indies will always prevent this traffic being dropped."

(2) The second reason was political. The merchant service was in peace the training-ground and in war the hunting-ground for manning the British Navy; and the cessation of the Slave Trade, it was argued, would mean not only a substantial decrease in the British mercantile marine but also a corresponding increase in that of rival countries, particularly France, Britain's constant enemy throughout the eighteenth century. It would be folly, therefore, for Britain to abandon the Trade unless—a most improbable supposition—all other participants therein could be persuaded to do likewise. Nor was that the only political question at issue. The strength of

the British hold on the West Indies was regarded as of great strategic importance in the naval wars with France.

(3) The third reason was that those Englishmen who profited from the slave-system—retired or absentee proprietors, bankers, mortgagees, sugar-merchants—constituted a large and powerful " vested interest." The " West-Indians " were as notable, if not as notorious, an element in English politics and society as the " nabobs " from East India ; and behind them lay the weight of the commercial cities. The greatness of Liverpool, which has been described as the principal slaving-port in all Europe, was built up on the Trade. The Mayor of Bristol, as early as 1713, described it as the " great support of our people." Even London would be ruined, so Alderman Sawbridge hotly asserted in 1788, if the Trade were tampered with. And to all that must be added the influence, for what it was worth, of the innumerable individuals who took their pickings, direct or indirect, from the profits which the Trade brought home to England. They were huge profits. It has been called " the most lucrative trade the world has ever seen." It paid on the average at least 15 per cent. One slave-ship alone might bring in as much as £60,000 by a single successful voyage. It was calculated that, even if two out of every three ventures failed, the profit might still be substantial.

Singly or together, these reasons go far to

explain why successive British Governments and Parliaments continued to support the slave-system; why the acquisition of the *Asiento* was hailed as the greatest diplomatic triumph of its time; why war-ministers like Chatham took a special interest in the British settlements in West Africa; why admirals like Rodney and Nelson vehemently opposed the anti-Slavery movement. They also explain why Secretaries of State instructed Colonial Governors to oppose any local interference with the Slave Trade and why measures passed by colonial legislatures to check it, usually in the form of import-duties, were disallowed from time to time in London. Bitter things were said in the days of the American Revolution as to this particular example of imperial tyranny; and in Jefferson's first draft of the Declaration of Independence George III was charged with the crime of warring on the unoffending Africans and transporting them into slavery. But, though there were Americans, especially in the North, who supported those attempts at restriction on moral grounds, the main motive seems to have been a rising alarm at the danger to small white communities of uncontrolled black immigration, exemplified by slave-risings in the South and even a " Negro plot " in New York. For the planters, of course, the continuance of Slavery and of at least as much of the Trade as was needed to continue it seemed no less a " necessity " than to anyone in England; and Jefferson himself confessed that

the aforesaid clause in the Declaration was
" struck out in complaisance to South Carolina
and Georgia who had never attempted to restrain the importation of slaves and who on the
contrary wished to continue it. Our northern
brethren also, I believe, felt a little tender under
those censures ; for though their people had
very few slaves themselves, yet they had been
pretty considerable carriers of them to others."
But, if colonial motives for restricting the Trade
were mixed, the imperial motive for vetoing
restriction was single and plain. Lord Dart-
mouth, whose Evangelical piety was notorious
—the " one who wears a coronet and prays "
in Cowper's poem—put it bluntly enough. " We
cannot allow the colonies," he said in 1774 when
he was President of the Board of Trade, " to
check or discourage in any degree a traffic so
beneficial to the nation."

But, if the slave-system was thus sustained
by British public opinion, there were differences
in the attitude of individuals towards it ranging
from those who wholeheartedly supported it to
those who regarded it as a deplorable necessity.
And there were some who actively assailed it
and protested against its continuance. In his
Christian Directory, published in 1673, Richard
Baxter, the famous Nonconformist, while he
accepted Slavery if strictly regulated, denounced
the slave-hunters as " the common enemies of
mankind " ; and in 1680 a tract by Morgan
Godwyn, an Anglican clergyman from Oxford

who had gone out to Barbados, exposed the planters' brutal treatment of their slaves and described the Trade as " a cruelty capable of no palliation." About the same time Mrs. Aphra Benn, the novelist, who had lived in Surinam, published her *Oroonoko or the Royal Slave*, afterwards dramatized by Southerne, the first work in English literature since *Othello* with a black man for its hero, in which the savagery of the slave-trader and the slave-owner was contrasted with the nobility of the slave. Thenceforward, in one form or another, by preachers, philosophers, poets and pamphleteers, the slave-system was constantly decried. Locke's first *Treatise on Civil Government*, published in 1689, opened with these words : " Slavery is so vile and miserable an estate of man, and so directly opposite to the generous temper and courage of our nation, that it is hardly to be conceived that an ' Englishman,' much less a ' gentleman,' should plead for it." And the same note of irony was sounded more bitterly by Montesquieu in 1748 : " It is impossible for us to suppose these creatures to be men, because, allowing them to be men, a suspicion would follow that we ourselves are not Christians." Defoe directly assailed the Slave Trade in his *Reformation of Manners*. Thomson, Pope, Savage and Shenstone alluded in their poems to the miseries of enslavement. Bishop Hayter preached against the Trade in 1755, and in 1760 the better-known Bishop Warburton referred in the pulpit to " the vast multitudes yearly stolen from the opposite continent and sacrificed by the colonists to their great idol, the god of gain," and declared outright that " the infamous traffic for slaves directly infringes both divine and human law." But these were all expressions of individual opinion only, and they were words, not deeds. To one community alone, the Quakers, belongs the honour of having repudiated the slave-system and in deed as well as word. George Fox, their founder, had urged the " Friends " in Barbados in 1671 to mitigate the evils of Slavery by treating their slaves well and by setting them free " after certain years of servitude " : and in 1688 the German Quakers of Germantown in Pennsylvania raised the moral issue involved both in slave-trading and in slave-owning. " Those who steal or rob men and those who buy or purchase them, are they not all alike ? " In course of time this lead was followed by the Society as a whole. By exhortation, censure and warning most of those Quakers in England or the colonies who owned slaves or were connected with the Trade were gradually induced to give up both. In 1774 a decree of expulsion from the Society was passed on any Friend who persisted in having dealings with the Trade, and in 1776 manumission was similarly enforced on any Friend who still owned slaves.

Meanwhile, in England as in France, a new interest in the uncivilized peoples of the world was awakened by the travels and discoveries of

Dampier, Tasman, Anson, Cook and others. Accounts of their voyages were published and almost as widely read as *Robinson Crusoe* : and, while incidentally the facts of white contact with the coloured races, including the Slave Trade, were thus made better known, the general result was a strengthening and spreading of humanitarian ideas. It took, indeed, romantic and exaggerated forms. " Man Friday " came to life. Aborigines brought home by voyagers from distant seas were made much of in fashionable society ; and the conception of an ideal " state of nature," popularized by Rousseau, and of the " noble savage " who in natural goodness as in freedom was at least the equal of civilized man became a favourite topic of discussion in cultivated circles. With all its fallacies and crudities this movement of thought marks the dawn of a new epoch in world-history. It meant that the body of ideas which were to come to the front in the last quarter of the eighteenth century and to dominate the nineteenth were not limited in application to Europeans. The " rights of man " were not conditioned by a colour-bar. Blacks and browns and yellows had their place with whites in " the brotherhood of man." The humanitarian movement, in fact, was an essential part of the revolutionary movement, and not in theory only. High principles might be more slowly put in practice with respect to backward peoples, less able than French *citoyens* or Boston colonists or Bristol rioters to assert their claims themselves : but at any rate the worst injustice to which they were subjected could not long survive the passing of the *ancien régime*. With all the watchwords of the new era — man's " unalienable rights," " *liberté, egalité, fraternité*," " radical reform," " democracy "—Slavery made a discord too strident to be borne.

It was not so clear, of course, in the second half of the eighteenth century as it is to-day that the slave-system was doomed. It showed, indeed, a stubborn power of resistance to the new ideas, and the opening of the series of direct attacks on it, which, piece by piece and in one area after another, achieved its ultimate destruction, might have been long delayed if the actual practice of Slavery had been confined to the western side of the Atlantic. But from early days planters on holiday or retiring to live in England had made a habit of bringing their domestic slaves with them. And with the slaves other concrete evidence of what Slavery meant was thrust under Englishmen's eyes. Slaves sometimes ran away and were hunted through the streets. Slave-auctions were advertised in the newspapers. And to many Englishmen, unhardened by colonial life, it seemed that, whatever might happen in the colonies, these things ought not to be allowed in England. Could English law permit the first principles of personal freedom to be set so utterly at naught on English soil ? For a time the answer to that question was in doubt. The Court of Common Pleas had admitted a slave to be a slave in England because he was a heathen; but Chief Justice Holt had expressed an opinion that " as soon as a Negro comes into England he becomes free "; and it was argued that at least those slaves who had become Christians could not legally be held in slavery in England nor carried back by force to the plantations. So uncertain was the position and so alarming the ease with which runaway slaves could get baptized that in 1729 the " West Indian " community appealed for an opinion to the Law Officers of the Crown, Yorke and Talbot. They declared that neither residence in England nor baptism affected the master's " right and property " in his slave and that the master could " legally compel him to return again to the plantations." In 1749, Yorke, as Lord Chancellor Hardwicke, confirmed this judgment. And there the matter rested till the entry into the field of the first of the " Abolitionists."

Granville Sharp was born in 1735, son of an archdeacon of Northumberland and grandson of an Archbishop of York. Only his two eldest brothers pursued the family vocation, one of them, John, succeeding to his father's office. Of the rest, two brothers and two sisters made their homes in London, where James, an ironmonger, became a wealthy and influential merchant of the City and William, a surgeon, was rewarded for a successful practice with the honour of a surgeonship to the King. But it was not their commercial or professional careers that made the " good Sharps " pleasantly notorious in the London world. A singularly close-knit family, their strongest tie was a passion for music ; and, all being well, they forgathered every evening to sup and practise together. William played the organ and the French horn, James the " jointed serpent," John (when in town) the 'cello, and Granville (who engraved his seal with G$\sharp$) the flute and the oboe. To the sisters, it seems, was left the piano or spinet. All of them sàng " at sight." On Sundays they entertained their friends with performances of sacred music, choral and orchestral, mainly devoted to Handel and usually concluding with the " Hallelujah Chorus." Notable members of Society were often among their guests—Lord North, Lord Sandwich, General Paoli, Goldsmith, Garrick, Mrs. Sheridan—and their fame reached its climax when brother William, bent on combining the pleasures of music and travel, designed a barge or house-boat, the *Apollo*, on which the family and their instruments were towed by horse along the Thames and other waterways near London, wafting their music across the meadows. On one occasion, in 1770, as they floated past Windsor Castle, they surprised King George sitting under a tree near the river and treated him to a concert for over an hour and a half.

" Little Greeny," as Granville was called in

his youth, was not the least original member of this original family. The twelfth of fourteen children, he had to forgo the costly education needed for the Church, and at the age of fifteen, after a short course at Durham Grammar School, he was sent to London and apprenticed to a linen-draper. At the end of seven years' service under three successive masters he entered a manufacturing business, but it promptly failed; and thereupon he turned his back on drapery and accepted a safe but obscure and unremunerative appointment as a junior civil servant in the Ordnance Office at the Tower. Neither shop nor office afforded much scope for the exertion of his natural ability or the cultivation of his tastes; and it was in his spare time—in reading and writing, in argumentation with his friends, and, of course, in the family circle—that he lived his real life. The family vein of eccentricity betrayed itself quite early in the zest and ingenuity with which he interpreted the prophecies in the books of Daniel and Revelation—a lifelong interest and in old age almost an obsession. Another oddity was his belief in the ancient institution of "frankpledge." It was, he was convinced, of Mosaic origin and, if revived in England, would constitute an ideal system of local self-government and national defence. But Granville had too much sagacity and too much humour to be a crank; and the curious thing about his other interests and activities was not so much the subject of them as the intellectual audacity with which he pursued them. On a sudden impulse he would throw himself with an easy confidence at the most formidable tasks. Before he was out of his 'teens, finding himself baffled in theological argument among his fellow-apprentices by a Socinian and a Jew who took their stand on the Greek and Hebrew texts of the Bible, he set himself to master both Greek and Hebrew—an achievement which asserted itself later on in the publication of learned tracts on the use of the definitive article in the Greek Testament, on the purity of the Hebrew texts of Ezra and Nehemiah, and on the syntax and pronunciation of the Hebrew tongue. No sooner, again, had the young apprentice discovered that the second of his masters had a claim to the barony of Willoughby de Perham than he not only embarked on a detailed study of his case but expounded it with a force which carried the worthy Mr. Willoughby straight into the House of Lords. No task, apparently, was too difficult for this remarkable young man to undertake if it came his way.

One day in 1765, as he was leaving his brother's surgery in Mincing Lane, he chanced to observe among the poor patients waiting at the door for free treatment a Negro whose appearance was so " extremely distressful " that he turned back to ask his brother about him. The Negro's name, it appeared, was Jonathan Strong, and he belonged to a Mr. David Lisle, an irascible lawyer from Barbados, by whom he had been flogged

48

so savagely that he could hardly walk, beaten on the head with a pistol so that he was nearly blind, and finally, since in this condition he was no longer of any use, turned out into the street. William and Granville did what they could for him. They secured his admission into St. Bartholomew's Hospital, and, when after four months' treatment he was discharged, they looked after him till his health was quite restored and then found a job for him as errand-boy at a chemist's shop in Fenchurch Street. And there the story of Jonathan Strong might have ended. The episode had not planted in Granville's mind any idea of questioning the old-established institution of Slavery. He had treated it as a matter of private charity. He soon forgot the whole affair, even the slave's name. And then, two years later, there was another accidental meeting. Lisle saw Strong in the street, followed him to the chemist's, observed that his property had recovered its value, and sold it for £30 to a Jamaica planter, James Kerr. To make sure of his purchase, Kerr promptly kidnapped Strong and entrusted him to the jailer at Poultry Corner prison for safekeeping till the next ship sailed to the West Indies. Terrified at the doom awaiting him, Strong contrived to get a desperate appeal for help conveyed to Granville, who at once consulted his brother, James, now a person of importance in the City, and went with him to the prison. Having elicited the whole story from the trembling

49

Negro, Granville warned the jailer not to surrender his charge without warrant. He then interviewed the Lord Mayor and asked him to summon before him anyone who claimed possession of Strong. In due course, accordingly, Kerr's attorney and Captain Laird, the master of the ship that was to take Strong to Jamaica, appeared before the Lord Mayor, presented the bill of sale, and claimed the slave. But the Lord Mayor held that no person, slave or free, could rightfully be imprisoned if no offence were alleged against him. He therefore discharged Strong, and, when Laird laid hold on him outside the court, Granville, prompted by a friendly lawyer, threatened to charge the captain with assault unless he released his hold. Laird withdrew and Strong was free.

Lisle and Kerr decided to leave him alone until they had punished and disarmed the busybody who had prevented them from doing what slave-owners had long been accustomed to do. They consulted their lawyers and began an action for damages to the tune of £200. Sharp's lawyers advised him not to fight the case. They showed him the opinion of Yorke and Talbot and informed him that no less an authority than Lord Mansfield, the Chief Justice, had more than once confirmed that opinion in the King's Bench. He would be wise, they said, to settle the dispute out of court on the best terms he could get and leave the Negro to his fate. But Sharp's blood was up. He knew nothing of the law beyond what he had gleaned in the peerage case, but what of that ? He coolly told the lawyers that " he could not believe the law of England was really so injurious to natural rights as so many great lawyers for political reasons had been pleased to assert," that he was not so " intimidated " as they were by the " opinion," and that he would study the law-books and construct his own defence. And so he did. Neither the technical difficulties nor the length of labour needed —still less a fiery challenge to a duel from Lisle —affected his resolve. For two years he toiled at the books and the result was a lengthy memorandum, resuscitating Holt's judgement and supporting it with an exposition of the principles of villeinage and the common law. He submitted it to the great Dr. Blackstone who had himself quoted Holt's opinion in his famous *Commentaries* ; but Blackstone, who was well aware of Mansfield's views, had omitted the dangerous passage from the last edition of his book, and, though at first he did not impugn Sharp's case but merely warned him that " it would be uphill work in the Court of King's Bench," and though he allowed himself to be retained together with the Solicitor-General and the Recorder of London for Sharp's defence, nevertheless, when it came to a formal consultation, he agreed with his colleagues that the case could not be fought. And yet, in a sense, Sharp won it. He had twenty copies of his memorandum made and sent them to eminent lawyers with such unsettling effects on professional opinion in general that Lisle's and Kerr's advisers shrank from continuing their suit and were ultimately fined treble costs for dropping it. In an introduction to *The Injustice and dangerous Tendency of tolerating Slavery in England,* under which title Sharp published his memorandum in 1769, he allowed himself one parting shot. He warned Lisle, Kerr and others concerned that, though he did not intend to take action, it was their freedom, not Strong's, that was in jeopardy, since they had violated " the Statutes of Provission and Premunire made 16th of K. Rich. II."

Sharp was not satisfied with his triumph. The law remained uncertain. He was determined to force his version of it on the courts and so to abolish Slavery in England. For the bitter opposition he would arouse among the powerful " West Indian " community he cared little ; for he knew that the great traditions of English law would be unaffected by social or political influence. His main difficulty was the attitude of the Lord Chief Justice. Mansfield had read the memorandum with an uneasy suspicion that it told the legal truth. If that should be established by a trial of the question on a straight issue, the consequences dismayed him. The humiliating reversal of the highest legal opinion, including his own, by an obscure layman was the least of the evils he foresaw. Trusting in that high opinion, hundreds of planters had brought their slaves to England. There were now between 14,000 and 15,000 of them in the country. A decision in Sharp's favour would mean that the owners would be deprived at a stroke of property worth roughly £700,000, and that the freed slaves would be set adrift without any means apart from charity for their maintenance. Mansfield, therefore, was as anxious to prevent as Sharp was to secure the straight issue being tried ; and a sort of duel ensued between the Lord Chief Justice and the junior civil servant. What Sharp needed was a repetition of the Strong case, and in 1770 he thought he had obtained it when a runaway slave, named Lewis, was recaptured by his master, Mr. Stapylton, and forcibly put on board a ship bound for Jamaica. The ship left London before Sharp could take action, but he caught it at Portsmouth with a writ of *habeas corpus,* and, when Lewis and Stayplton appeared in the Court of King's Bench, he seemed in sight of victory. But Mansfield was not easily to be beaten. He refused to consider the broader question until it had been proved that Lewis was in fact Stapylton's property and he obtained from the jury a verdict that he was not. He concluded the proceedings with a warning addressed to Lewis' counsel, the brilliant Whig barrister, Dunning, but evidently meant for Sharp.

I don't know what the consequences may be if the masters were to lose their property by accidentally bringing their slaves to England. I hope it never will be finally discussed ; for I would have all masters think them free and all Negroes think they were not, because then they would both behave better.

In the course of the next two years three more slaves were rescued, but in circumstances in which a judgement on the straight issue could not be obtained, and then in 1772 Mansfield was cornered at last. The case of James Somerset, who had been brought to England by his master, Charles Stewart, from Virginia, and had run away, been recaptured, and shipped for sale in Jamaica was the same as Lewis' except that he was undoubtedly Stewart's property. The "West Indians" on their side had been so harassed by Sharp's campaign that they were now almost as anxious as he was to have the uncertain question of their rights decided. They subscribed the money required for the costs of the case, and this time they enlisted Dunning on their side. But, however ably his own old opinion might be argued, Mansfield was now quite convinced that it was wrong. All he could do was to try to prevent his being forced to admit it. He twice adjourned the case. He repeatedly recommended its abandonment. He solemnly warned the parties concerned of the probable effects of their obstinacy. He invited Stewart to end the dispute by setting Somerset free. He urged both sides to settle it out of court. He suggested that their proper course was to ask Parliament to legislate.

But if the parties will have it decided, we must

ABOLITION OF SLAVERY IN BRITISH ISLES

give an opinion. Compassion will not on the one hand nor inconvenience on the other be to decide, but the law. . . . If the parties will have judgement, " *fiat justitia, ruat coelum.*"

It was no use. In the rising excitement of the crowded court—for public interest in the matter was now keen—the case went on to its conclusion. On June 22 Mansfield delivered his judgement. " The power claimed never was in use here nor acknowledged by the law. . . . The state of Slavery . . . is so odious that nothing can be suffered to support it but positive law. Whatever inconveniences therefore may follow from the decision, I cannot say this case is allowed or approved by the law of England ; and therefore the black must be discharged."

This judgement was limited to the question of forcibly retaining possession of a slave, but its implicit extension to all a slave-owner's " rights " was obvious, and from that time all slaves in England, whether or not they chose to remain in their old masters' service, were recognized as free men. To Ireland also the judgement automatically applied, and in Scotland the issue was decided in the similar case of Joseph Knight in 1778, the Scottish judges taking the broader ground that the master's right of dominion was in general unsustained by law.

Thus, mainly as the outcome of one man's work, Slavery was deleted from the British Isles. And that was not all Granville Sharp had done. The Somerset Case marks the beginning of the

end of Slavery throughout the British Empire.
For behind the legal judgement lay the moral
judgement ; and, however different the circumstances on the farther side of the Atlantic
and whatever other arguments might be adduced,
it seemed to the growing number of Englishmen
who were now thinking about it that only an
illogical morality could outlaw Slavery in Britain
because it was so " odious " and tolerate it on
British soil overseas where the mass of the slaves
were far worse treated. Granville Sharp, in
fact, had initiated a movement which was to
proceed, slowly at times but continuously and
inexorably, to its ultimate triumph in 1833.

① Quakers.
⑪ Sharpe.

CHAPTER III

THE EMANCIPATORS

THE immediate sequel of the Somerset Case was the opening of a new series of individual attacks on the slave-system, of which two were delivered by two of the greatest men of the age. In 1774, when the Evangelical Movement was rising to its height, John Wesley published his *Thoughts upon Slavery*. His colleague, Whitefield, who died in 1770, had been so eager to advance the economic prosperity of Georgia and so sure that "hot countries cannot be cultivated without Negroes" that he had joyfully acclaimed in 1751 the withdrawal of the ban which had kept the young colony clean of slaves. But to Wesley, who had studied the details of the Slave Trade and closely followed the arguments in the Somerset Case, no material considerations could justify the injustice and cruelty of the slave-system : and with characteristic fervour he called on slave-traders and slave-owners to look into their consciences and spill no more innocent blood. Very different in manner and objective was Adam Smith's attack. In a few dry sentences in the *Wealth of Nations*, published in 1776, he struck at the economic roots of Slavery

by arguing that it did not pay. " It appears
from the experience of all ages and nations that
the work done by freemen comes cheaper in the
end than that performed by slaves." Nor were
hard facts wanting to support these appeals to
conscience and common sense. Robertson's
History of America, which appeared in 1777 and
was widely read, described the growth of Negro
Slavery in South America ; and several English
translations of the Abbé Raynal's *Histoire des
deux Indes*, which contained a minute account
of the slave-system, were published between
1776 and 1783. From these and many minor
sources educated Englishmen were learning more
and more about Slavery and becoming for the
most part more and more averse to it. And this
development of public opinion was by no means
confined to social idealists or religious " enthu-
siasts." No one was a more typical Tory of the
old school than Dr. Johnson and no one hated
Slavery more fiercely. He was deeply interested
in the Knight Case and dictated to Boswell, who
did not share his views, an argument on the case,
based on the premiss that " no man is by nature
the property of another." But it was no mere
point of law, it was a passionate humanity that
inflamed Johnson's mind not only against the
slave-system but against the colonists who practised it. It embittered his notorious antagonism
to the American Revolution. " How is it," he
asked in *Taxation no Tyranny*, " that we hear
the loudest yelps for liberty among the drivers

of Negroes?" And "upon one occasion,"
records Boswell, "when in company with some
very grave men at Oxford, his toast was ' Here's
to the next insurrection of the Negroes in the
West Indies.'"

Acts teach more than words, and, just as the
conduct of David Lisle led straight to the
Somerset judgement, so it may well be that a
ghastly incident which occurred in 1781 had
more effect on public opinion than all the teach-
ing and preaching of the time. As the slave-
ship _Zong_ was on its way from West Africa to
Jamaica, sickness broke out among the 400
slaves on board. Alarmed by the prospect of
more than the normal number of deaths, the
captain, Luke Collingwood, bethought him of a
clause in the insurance policy under which the
insuring company had to bear the loss of any
part of the cargo jettisoned to save the rest ;
and on the false pretext of a shortage of water
he ordered 132 of the sicklier slaves to be thrown
overboard. In due course the case came up for
trial in London. The issue, however, was not
one of murder, but simply as to whether the act
of jettison was in fact necessary and who accordingly should pay for it. " So far from the charge
of murder lying against these people," said the
Solicitor-General who was briefed by the ship's
owners, " there is not the least imputation, of
cruelty I will not say, but of impropriety, not
the least ! " And Mansfield himself, in com-
menting on the case, declared that there was

"no doubt, though it shocks one very much, that the case of slaves was the same as if horses had been thrown overboard." Shocking indeed it was, and apparently irremediable. Granville Sharp, it need hardly be said, had fastened on the case and in 1783 he submitted a full review of it to the Admiralty and to the Duke of Portland, then head of the Fox-North Coalition, appealing for the initiation of a trial for murder. But this time he could not refute the accepted interpretation of the law. The only remedy lay in new legislation, and for that neither Government nor Parliament was ready.

Meanwhile the whole question had been directly affected by the American Revolution. The separation of the thirteen insurgent colonies from the mother-country, recognized in the peace-treaty of 1783, meant that a section of the slave-system had been cut clean out of the British Empire : the owners of some 600,000 slaves had discarded their allegiance to King George. The vast majority of these American slave-owners were planters of the South, and their ideas and emotions about Slavery were by no means shared in the North, where, long before the rupture with the mother-country, a vigorous body of anti-Slavery opinion had grown up. American Quakers had kept step with English Quakers. Anthony Benezet (1713–84), an exiled Huguenot who had joined the Friends and taken charge of their school at Philadelphia, was particularly active in denouncing Slavery and the Trade. He published several pamphlets on the subject and corresponded with such fellow-workers in the cause on the other side of the Atlantic as Sharp, Wesley and Raynal. In 1783, not long before his death, he wrote to " Charlotte, Queen of Great Britain," beseeching her compassion for " the miseries under which so large a part of mankind are suffering the most unjust and grievous oppression." Outside religious circles the most effective assault on the slave-system was probably the brief but trenchant tract on *African Slavery in America*, published by Thomas Paine at Philadelphia in 1775, in which, agreeing with Johnson on this point if not on any other, he asked Americans " to consider with what consistency or decency they complain so loudly of attempts to enslave them while they hold so many hundred thousands in slavery." A month after this tract appeared, the first American anti-Slavery Society was founded at Philadelphia. In the following year it was resolved by the Revolutionary Congress " that no slaves be imported into any of the thirteen United Colonies." And by 1778 laws prohibiting importation had been passed in Rhode Island, Connecticut, Pennsylvania, Delaware and Virginia. But it was still legal in 1783 for citizens of New England or the Middle States to take a hand in importing slaves into the plantation-States of the South where Slavery was now as deeply rooted as in any West Indian island. Eighty years later, it was still so deeply rooted there that, rather than allow it to be torn up, its practitioners were ready to fight a second war of secession which threatened to split the American Republic as the first had split the British Empire. Obviously, therefore, the withdrawal of so stubborn a body of slave-owners from British citizenship in 1783 considerably lightened the task of the anti-Slavery campaigners in Britain. It was difficult enough, as will be seen, to overcome the opposition of the West Indian " interest " to the abolition of the Slave Trade : it would have been still more difficult if the representatives of the American " South " had fought beside the representatives of the West Indies. It seems certain, therefore, that the abolition of the British Slave Trade would have been delayed if the American Revolution had not occurred ; and it is interesting, if idle, to speculate what would have happened when the British Parliament went on to abolish Slavery—a far more drastic interference with colonial liberties than Stamp Acts or Tea Duties.

The American Revolution had another effect on the course of the anti-Slavery movement in England. The loss of the thirteen colonies compelled British statesmen to examine and reorganize "what was left" of the old Empire. The reform of British rule in India, for example, was largely due to the fact that the American secession had swung the commercial balance of the Empire over from West to East. Better government in India, it was thought, would mean better

Trusteeship Principle.

trade. But there was also a moral side to it. This was the time of Burke's passionate championship of Indian wrongs and of his historic declaration that British rule in India was in the nature of a " trust " on behalf of the Indian people : it was the time of Warren Hastings' impeachment. And Pitt was sincere enough when he stated that one motive of his great India Bill of 1784 was to render the British connexion " a blessing to the native Indians." The days of the " nabobs " were over ; and henceforward it was recognized in principle, and commonly, if by no means invariably, in practice, that commercial contact with backward peoples involved moral responsibilities. Humanitarianism had entered // British politics.

In the West Indies, however, the material and the moral arguments for reform, concordant in India, were in conflict. The loss of the American colonies accentuated the economic value of the " sugar islands " and intensified, as the conduct of the war with France was soon to show, the desire to acquire more of them. But, so far from implying any change in the relations between whites and blacks, this rendered the maintenance of the slave-system more of an economic " necessity " than ever. Nor on the morrow of defeat, when Britain's first task was to husband her national strength, had the old point about the mercantile marine lost any of its force. Thus, in high political circles, throughout the American War and at its close, there was no sign of any weakening in the traditional attitude to the slave-system. When, in 1776, Mr. David Hartley, member for Hull, proposed, and Sir George Saville, member for Yorkshire, seconded, a motion against the Slave Trade, the House of Commons straightway threw it out; and when, in 1783, the Quakers presented a petition for the abolition of the Trade, Lord North commended the humanity that prompted it, " but still," he said, " he was afraid that it would be found impossible to abolish the Slave Trade . . . for it was a trade which had in some measure become necessary to almost every nation in Europe; and, as it would be next to an impossibility to induce them all to give it up, so he was apprehensive that the wishes of the humane petitioners could not be accomplished."

But if the material arguments on the Trade's behalf had been strengthened by events, so also had the moral arguments against it. The new philanthropy could not be limited to one race or country. Consciences stirred on behalf of Asiatics could not ignore the claims of Africans, nor fail to recognize, as soon as the facts were examined, that all the injuries inflicted in a few years of misgovernment on the people of Bengal were almost negligible in comparison with what Slavery and the Trade had done to the Negroes for generations past and were still doing every day. Could those who championed the one cause, could Burke or Fox or Pitt forget the other? And outside politics a psychological impulse was now at work from which Slavery could not escape. Many Englishmen had regarded the American War as not only a blunder but a crime. Granville Sharp, for instance, had resigned his post at the Ordnance Office rather than take a share, however small, in providing the implements of fratricide. That crime had brought its own punishment; but men of deep religious feeling, especially among the Evangelicals, were still haunted by a sense of national misdoing, by a conviction, so to speak, of national sin; and of all such national sins the slave-system in its flat defiance of every Christian principle was manifestly the worst. It is significant that Dr. Paley, whose religion was not of the emotional kind, suggested in his *Principles of Morals*, published in 1785, that the secession of the colonies may have been designed by Providence to bring an end to Slavery.

Now that this contest and the passions which attend it are no more, there may succeed perhaps a season for reflecting whether a legislature, which had so long lent its assistance to the support of an institution replete with human misery, was fit to be trusted with an empire.

A post-war renaissance, a period of new men and measures and of imperial reconstruction, an invasion of philanthropy into politics, a growing consciousness among earnest men of the moral responsibilities of the state—such were the circumstances in which the first organized attack on the British slave-system was launched.

Again it was the Quakers who began it. In 1783 a standing committee of six—William Dillwyn, George Harrison, Samuel Hoare, Thomas Knowles, John Lloyd and Joseph Woods—was appointed to carry on continuous work by personal influence and by the publication of books and newspaper-articles " for the relief and liberation of the Negro slaves in the West Indies and for the discouragement of the Slave Trade on the coast of Africa." In 1784, this committee collaborated with the " Meeting for Sufferings " in preparing a pamphlet on *The Case of our fellow-creatures, the oppressed Africans*, which was sent to every member of Parliament and various notabilities ; and in 1785 a tract by Anthony Benezet on the treatment of slaves in British colonies was similarly circulated in political quarters and in the public-schools. Round this Quaker nucleus a group of individual assailants of the slave-system soon began to cluster. The first of them, of course, was Granville Sharp who, since the Somerset Case, had corresponded with all the bishops and obtained from most of them a promise of sympathy and from some of active support for a campaign against the Trade. The next recruit was James Ramsay, a clergyman who had served for nineteen years in the island of St. Christopher and was now devoting the spare hours of his life in a Kentish vicarage to a series of outspoken pamphlets depicting and denouncing West Indian slavery as he had seen it. And then came Thomas Clarkson who was to do as much as any man to secure the triumph of the cause. Son of the clerical headmaster of Wisbech Grammar School, he was educated at St. Paul's, where he obtained an exhibition enabling him to go on to Cambridge; and in 1785 he won the University prize for a Latin Essay on the theme *Is it Right to make Men Slaves against their Will?* In composing it he had gleaned what facts he could about the Slave Trade, and, as he rode back to London after reading the essay in the Senate House, he found his mind dwelling on the subject.

Clarkson's "Conversion".

I became at times very seriously affected while upon the road. I stopped my horse occasionally and dismounted and walked. I frequently tried to persuade myself in these intervals that the contents of my essay could not be true. The more, however, I reflected upon them or rather upon the authorities on which they were founded, the more I gave them credit. Coming in sight of Wades Mill in Hertfordshire, I sat down disconsolate on the turf by the roadside and held my horse. Here a thought came into my mind that, if the contents of the essay were true, it was time some person should see these calamities to their end.

When he came to prepare an English version of his essay for publication, this conviction grew on him; and when presently he met Dillwyn and Granville Sharp and Ramsay, he made up his mind not only to collaborate with them but

to abandon the clerical career he had begun and
devote the whole of his life to the Abolitionist
cause. It was a noble decision; for Clarkson,
unlike some of his colleagues, was a poor man
who could ill afford to spend his days in pure
philanthropy. And it was an historic decision;
for without Clarkson's unflagging enthusiasm
and industry, his personal researches and propaganda all over the country, and the prestige and
authority he presently attained, the attack on
the British slave-system could not have achieved
its object as quickly or as fully as it did.

The time was now ripe for a consolidation of
the Abolitionist forces, and on May 22, 1787, a
committee of twelve was formed, including the
Quaker Committee (except Knowles) and Clarkson, with Sharp as chairman. Its declared
object was to procure and publish " such information as may tend to the abolition of the Slave
Trade," and for this limited purpose it was
sufficiently equipped with men and money. But
to elucidate and exhibit the facts, to do for the
Slave Trade what the long and detailed reports
of parliamentary committees had done for Bengal, was only the first and easier half of the
Abolitionist campaign. The second and harder
half was to secure the support of Parliament.
There was nothing illegal in the Slave Trade;
it could only be abolished by new legislation:
and to persuade Parliament to contemplate an
Abolition Act may well have seemed a desperate
task in 1787. No member of it had supported

Hartley and Saville in 1776 or contested North's assumptions in 1783 : and in 1785, when another petition against the Trade was presented on behalf of the inhabitants of Bridgwater by its members, Poulet and Hood, they had reported to their constituents that "there did not appear the least disposition to pay any further attention to it." Why was this ? The House was not impervious to moral appeals. As the debates on the India Bills had already shown and those on the impeachment of Warren Hastings were about to show, there were men of philanthropic feeling on both sides and on both front benches. Why were Burke and Fox and Pitt so vocal about India and so silent about Africa ? Burke's conduct is especially significant. He had felt, he was bound to feel, the wrongs of the slave-system, and in 1780 he had actually drafted a Bill for ameliorating the treatment of slaves, making provision for their moral and mental advancement, and so preparing the way for the ultimate abolition of Slavery and the Trade together ; but he had not, and for twelve years he did not, make it public. His reason or excuse for this delay was that in 1780 " an abolition of the Slave Trade would have appeared a very chimerical object." In blunter terms it was impossible in 1780, and even in the more liberal atmosphere of 1787 it was still impossible, for a front-rank politician to espouse that particular cause without jeopardizing not only his own career but also the future of his party. For the representatives of those commercial, financial and political interests which, though not opposed to measures for improving the government of India, would obstinately resist an attack on the slave-system, sat on both sides of the House. Can Burke or Fox be blamed, then, for not committing themselves to a crusade which must have split the Whigs and wrecked their chance of achieving the aims on which they were united ? And Pitt was in the same dilemma with the Tories. Yet, unless a parliamentarian of calibre comparable to theirs could be found to do what they could not, the cause of Abolition would still remain chimerical. Parliament was far less responsible to public opinion then than now ; and, however well the Abolition Committee did its work of education and appeal outside its walls, the same work had to be done inside them. For that work someone was needed who was not a leader of either party and so could draw votes from each, someone more influential and persuasive and popular than a Hartley or a Hood, someone who could force the facts on members' minds without losing their attention and invoke their consciences without giving them offence. By a remarkable coincidence just such a man was available just at that time.

William Wilberforce was born at Hull in 1759. Coming of an old Yorkshire family which had prospered in business, he was enabled, more fortunate than Granville Sharp, to finish his education at Cambridge and to drift on to a leisured life in London. Small, slender, frail, so short-sighted that the peering posture of his body was likened as time went on to the letter S, with a whimsical face which would almost have been ugly but for the brilliant deep-set eyes, sensitive but not shy, never still and rarely silent, he possessed all the gifts—the oddity and charm, the unselfconsciousness, the flow of witty conversation, the drawing-room accomplishments of mimicry and song, the wholehearted love of amusement—which the fashionable world required of its favourites. His personal magnetism, his unforced interest in everybody and everything, his utter lack of malice, soon made him hosts of friends ; but there was one friendship which he valued more than all the rest together. Pitt was the same age and had been at Cambridge in his time, but Wilberforce first got to know him listening to the debates on the American War in the gallery of the House of Commons and discussing them afterwards at the clubs. Acquaintance quickly ripened into intimacy. For some years they were the closest friends, living together at Wilberforce's house at Wimbledon, taking their holidays together, elected to Parliament together in 1780, Pitt for Appleby, Wilberforce for Hull ; and, when Pitt became Prime Minister in 1783,[4] there was no one on whom he could more certainly rely for support in speech and vote than Wilberforce. The brilliant young Yorkshireman, though not perhaps of the heavier metal of which Cabinet

Ministers are made, had soon proved himself an excellent debater with an unusual gift of natural eloquence and a voice so beautiful in range and tone as to earn him the nickname of " the nightingale of the House."

But in 1784–5 Wilberforce underwent an experience which threatened to terminate his political career. Under the influence of Isaac Milner, once an usher at his school, now a Cambridge " don," and soon to be famous as President of Queens, holder of Newton's chair of mathematics and Dean of Carlisle, he was suddenly engulfed in the deep current of religious emotion which Wesley had set flowing far and wide through the English working and middle classes but which had so far made little way in the cooler or more cynical circles of fashionable society. The process of " conversion " was completed under the stern hand of John Newton who had served, as it chanced, as captain of a slave-ship before his own " conversion " had led him to the Church and to the ministry, and now, after a curacy at Olney which had brought him into contact with the unhappy Cowper, was preaching to crowded congregations at St. Mary Woolnoth's in the City on the terrors of sin and hell. Wilberforce emerged from this experience a changed man. He was possessed now with a sense of the nearness and goodness of God which never left him all the rest of his long life. And though by normal standards his previous conduct had been above reproach, his old habits and interests and amusements seemed in the light of his new conscience not merely frivolous but almost sinful. Clubs, race-meetings, dances, the theatre, all were put away. And Pitt, who had watched his friend's spiritual adventure with sympathetic anxiety, was distressed to learn that, disquieted now by the dubious methods and ambitions of party politics, he was thinking of resigning his seat in Parliament. Pitt pleaded with him, urged that solitude and seclusion from practical affairs were not a necessary part of Christian duty, and ultimately persuaded him to resume in some measure his social and political activities. But the life had gone out of it all; and it seems probable that Wilberforce would not have stayed long in politics if the shadow of the Slave Trade had not fallen across his path. He heard about it first from Ramsay. He discussed it with Ramsay's friend and patron, Lord Middleton and his public-spirited wife. He listened to Newton's remorseful and lurid descriptions of his earlier life. He read Clarkson's book, sent for the author, and begged for further information. He was soon convinced that the Slave Trade ought to be stopped, and soon realized that it could not be stopped unless someone took up the cause in Parliament. It was a cause, moreover, which appealed to his new-found conscience, untainted by party interest, involving the moral and physical welfare of countless human beings, a challenge to a Christian and a patriot to redeem his country from sin, a real crusade. To Wilberforce the idea of taking up this cause seemed providential : and so in a sense it seemed to Pitt. Sitting one day in the summer of 1787 with Wilberforce and Grenville under an old oak above the vale of Keston, Pitt brought the question to a head. " Why don't you, Wilberforce," he asked, " give notice of a motion on the subject of the Slave Trade ? "

From that moment Wilberforce started on a road which was to lead him to a fame as great as that of any of his famous contemporaries. The abolition of the British slave-system and the consolidation of the British humanitarian tradition have been mainly associated with his name. But he was always the first to insist that he shared the credit of those achievements with other men. Buxton's work will be dealt with later. At these earlier stages Clarkson's contribution was no less indispensable. But Clarkson, though Wilberforce's close and constant collaborator, was not one of the group of intimate friends on whom Wilberforce chiefly depended for the intellectual and spiritual sympathy and help he needed. Chief among these was Henry Thornton (1760–1815), banker and M.P. for Southwark for thirty-two years. Thornton had inherited the wealth which his grandfather had made in the Russian trade, and had inherited also from his father, John Thornton, a habit of munificent charity. John had spent widely in endowing schools, providing for poor scholars,

assisting needy clergymen and buying up livings
for their occupation, St. Mary Woolnoth's, for
example, for John Newton. Henry gave away
in similar " good works " no less than six-
sevenths of his income till he married, and after
that at least one-third of it. " Tall and stately,"
as a contemporary described him, he seems at
this distance a rather formidable figure, cold,
austere, Olympian : but Wilberforce was devoted to him, and there was nobody on whose
judgement he and his allies more implicitly relied.
From 1792 to 1797 Wilberforce lived in his house
in Clapham, three miles from Westminster and
then a quiet country village, and the big oval
library of the house, designed by Chatham, became the regular haunt of the Abolitionists.
Another neighbour was Granville Sharp, the
father of the Abolitionist movement, the patri-
arch of the Clapham brethren, and their " abid-
ing guest and bosom friend." But as Sharp
grew older, he became more and more obsessed
by his " prophecies "—he once lectured Fox on
the meaning of the " Little Horn " in Daniel—
and, while his name and fame and stainless character were no small asset to the Abolitionist
cause, its practical ends were better served as
time went on by another of the older members
of the Chatham group, Charles Grant (1746–1823),
who lived next door to Thornton. Entering the
East India Company's service in early life, he
was singled out by Governor-General Cornwallis
from all his contemporaries for his meticulous

honesty and his capable handling of commercial
policy. After attaining high office in Bengal,
he retired to England, joined the Company's
Court of Directors, and in 1805 became its chairman—a post of great power and responsibility.
From 1802 to 1818 he sat in Parliament as member for Inverness-shire. Born in poverty and
poorly educated, he made his own way in the
world by his native ability and force of character, but what his friends admired in him more
than his masterful will and practical efficiency
was his simple, unpretentious goodness. " He
was one of the very best men I ever knew," said
Wilberforce. An Anglo-Indian colleague and
intimate friend of Grant was John Shore (1751–
1834), afterwards Lord Teignmouth, who, sharing Grant's religious convictions and his belief
that British rule in India was a matter of " strict
duty " towards the Indian peoples, found a
natural home at Clapham when he retired from
the Governor-Generalship in 1798. A nearer
contemporary of Wilberforce and Thornton was
James Stephen (1758–1832), who after ten years'
practice at the Bar in St. Christopher returned
to England and settled down at Clapham in 1794.
A friend of Perceval's, he was M.P. for Tralee
and East Grinstead from 1808 to 1815, but he
was an unpersuasive speaker, and his work for
the cause was mainly done outside Parliament,
in his published descriptions of the slave-system
and in arming Wilberforce with arguments and
facts. So deep indeed had the sights he had

seen in the West Indies bitten into Stephen's
soul that his talk and correspondence betrayed
at times a note of passion, a touch of acid, an
impatience of delay or compromise, which contrasted sharply with Wilberforce's gentleness or
Thornton's calm. Last but not least of the
central figures in the group comes Zachary
Macaulay (1768–1838), younger than the others,
but abreast with them all in the amount and
value of his work for the cause. Like Stephen,
he had been in the West Indies, having gone out
at the age of seventeen as under-manager of an
estate in Jamaica. His earlier letters home took
Slavery more or less for granted.

You would hardly know your friend with whom
you have spent so many hours in more peaceful and
more pleasant scenes, were you to view me in a
field of canes, amidst perhaps a hundred of the
sable race, cursing and bawling, while the noise of
the whip resounding on their shoulders and the
cries of the poor wretches would make you imagine
that some unlucky accident had carried you to the
doleful shades.

After four years of this work an offer of a post
in England enabled him to come home, and the
memory of his experience in Jamaica would
probably not have troubled his mind for long if
he had not been brought under the influence of
Thomas Babington, who had recently married
his sister. An English landowner of the best
type, master of Rothley Temple in Leicester-
shire, M.P. for the county-town for twenty years,

open-hearted and straightforward, in the highest
meaning of the words a simple-minded man,
Babington set himself to impart his own deep
sense of religion and of the purpose of life to his
somewhat conceited and worldly young brother-
in-law. The result was swift and profound.
Macaulay was changed like Wilberforce ; and,
anxious to share his benefactor's interests as well
as his faith, he threw himself into the Abolitionist
movement into which Babington had been drawn
by his friendship with Wilberforce. The young
zealot's personal acquaintance with Slavery was
useful enough, but still more useful was the remarkable power which he soon displayed—and
was presently to bequeath to his more famous
son—of hard and protracted brain-work, of
grasping and co-ordinating a multitude of detailed facts, and of remembering them. If his
colleagues in later days were ever at a loss on
some point, however small, " Let us look it up
in Macaulay," they would say. His portrait
shows a thin-lipped, rather narrow-eyed, broad-
browed face with a singularly still, almost inani-
mate expression, and—how unlike his son in
this !—he was notoriously stiff, taciturn, and,
when speech was needed, slow in fitting words
to thoughts. A chilling and unattractive personality, one might suppose, and yet there is
first-rate authority for saying that to know the
man well was to love him.

To this inner circle of the fraternity must be
added William Smith, M.P. for Norwich, full-

bodied, robust, given to loud laughter, an excellent foil to grave Thornton or silent Macaulay; Thomas Gisborne, who declined the parliamentary seat for Derby in favour of a Staffordshire parsonage and at whose house on the fringe of Needwood Forest Wilberforce was constantly renewing the intimate friendship of his Cambridge days; Edward Eliot, who was closely linked with Pitt as well as Wilberforce, and, if he had lived, would certainly have taken a leading part in the parliamentary fight for Abolition; Hannah More, entertaining Wilberforce on his honeymoon or coming up from her Somerset schools for a visit to Clapham; and always in the background, Isaac Milner, that "kind-hearted, talkative, wise old man." Presently, too, a second generation of "Claphamites" took its place in this community—the two young Grants, Robert and Charles, one destined to be Governor of Bombay, the other to be Secretary of State for the Colonies and Lord Glenelg; the two young Stephens, James and George, both of whom will figure prominently on later pages of this book; and, later on, young Tom Macaulay.

The popular title of this remarkable *coterie* was the "Clapham Sect"; an appropriate title, since, apart from the personal ties of friendship and marriage—Thornton was Wilberforce's first cousin, Babington married Macaulay's sister, Gisborne Babington's, Stephen Wilberforce's—the strongest link between them was their religion. Every Sunday the brethren gathered at the parish church to hear a sermon from John Venn (1789–1813), himself an active participant in all the Sect's humanitarian activities. And scarcely less appropriate was the half-mocking, half-respectful nickname given to those of the brethren who sat in Parliament—the " Saints." For it was their selfless devotion to high causes, their lack of all personal ambition, their scrupulous honesty and candour, their frank appeal to conscience and Christianity, that gave that little group a power in the House of Commons out of all proportion to its numbers or its parliamentary gifts. Only Wilberforce was an orator : Thornton, though his special knowledge of finance commanded attention in committee or in a consultation with the Cabinet, was as indifferent a speaker as Stephen or Macaulay. Nor did they owe anything to party interest. Most of them were " independents " on principle. Smith usually voted Whig and Stephen Tory. Wilberforce was first and last a " Pittite," but, though he could vote for Sidmouth too and thereby earn the hatred of the Radicals, his Pitt was always the young Pitt of 1783–93, the champion of Catholic Emancipation and " moderate " Reform. Thornton, again, though a friend and confidant of Pitt, often sided with Fox. It was, indeed, because of this independence and because it was known to be grounded on a refusal to obey the lesser loyalties of life, that the " Saints " were so great a force in Parliament and outside it. " A brotherhood of Christian politicians "—there has never been anything like it since.

Gifted as they all were, the central figure of the group, the man they felt to be their leader, was Wilberforce. " I am in hopes some good may come out of our Clapham system," wrote Thornton to Grant in 1793 : " Wilberforce is a candle that should not be hid under a bushel." And, as has been seen, it was Wilberforce's parliamentary talents that, linked with Clarkson's industry and the propaganda of the Abolitionist Committee, made it possible to open the great attack on the Slave Trade. But it must not be supposed that either Wilberforce or any of his collaborators were interested only in that one aspect of the humanitarian movement. To begin with, they had not forgotten Slavery itself, and their reason for deciding to deal first with the Trade was not only that it was the easier to destroy but the belief that its destruction would certainly and quickly bring to an end the whole slave-system which it supplied and sustained. Nor, again, were the Abolitionists only negative in their aims, only out to abolish. From the outset there was a positive side to their policy. It was not enough, they felt, to stop injuring the Africans : an attempt should be made to help them, to give them the best instead of the worst of what European civilization had to offer. And, since in the eyes of the " Saints " there was one gift incomparably more valuable than any other, it is natural to find them taking a leading part in the great new outburst of missionary enterprise at this period. The foundation of the Church Missionary Society in 1799 had been first discussed in Wilberforce's room : its first chairman was John Venn, its treasurer Thornton. Of the British and Foreign Bible Society, founded in 1804, Lord Teignmouth was the first president, Wilberforce vice-president, and Thornton again treasurer. And some of the other "Saints" served on the committees of these and other similar bodies such as the Religious Tract Society. The initial field of the work thus set on foot was India, and it was Wilberforce again who was mainly responsible for procuring the readier admission of missionaries into India in 1813 ; but before long the first British missionaries were beginning also to work and to die in "The White Man's Grave."

Christianity first, then commerce : for the Abolitionists believed that the growth of a "legitimate" European trade in West Africa would not only be of mutual benefit to Africans and Europeans but would tend to drive the Slave Trade out, because the chiefs would discover that the foreign goods they wanted could be got in exchange for other African products than human beings. Thus Wilberforce devoted part of his first speech against the Slave Trade, and so did Pitt, to the possibility of developing a more respectable British business in Africa. And, thirdly, colonization. Both for missionaries and for merchants some more permanent form of settlement was needed than the scattered huts and enclosures which sufficed for the purposes of the Slave Trade on the coast. But anything so ambitious as a "colony" would scarcely have been projected at this early date but for a peculiar sequence of events. The Somerset judgement, as Mansfield had foreseen, had produced an awkward social problem. Some of the freed slaves had remained as paid servants with their masters : some had found employment elsewhere : but several hundred of them had drifted into idleness and destitution. After 1783 the problem had been intensified by the demobilization of the Negroes who had served with the British forces in the American War and of whom some had been planted down in Nova Scotia, some in the Bahamas, and some in London. Relief of a kind was afforded by private charity. Granville Sharp himself maintained a growing number of personal pensioners, and in 1786 a committee "for relieving the black poor" was set up : but it was soon evident that the problem was more than it could cope with, and Sharp was already contemplating the idea of repatriation as the only effective solution, when a certain Dr. Sweatman, who had spent a few years as a naturalist in Sierra Leone, came forward with a definite suggestion that a colony of the Negro paupers should be founded in that part of Africa. The project bristled with difficulties, but Sharp embraced it with characteristic ardour ; and happily

Pitt's Government, which just at this time was trying to solve the problem of overcrowded gaols and hulks by transporting convicts to a colony at Botany Bay, was willing to encourage a similar method of getting rid of the "black poor." It provided a naval officer to take charge of the expedition, free transport for the Negroes, and six months' maintenance for the settlement. On May 9, 1787, some 400 Negroes were safely landed in St. George's Bay; a tract of twenty square miles on the coast was purchased from the local chief; and work was begun on the building of a town. In due course the control of the colony was vested in the Sierra Leone Company, "chartered" by Act of Parliament in 1791, of which Sharp was president, Thornton chairman, and Grant and Wilberforce among the first directors. Of the troubles which soon afflicted this unique experiment in philanthropic colonization—disease, desertion, attacks from without, rebellion within, and early in the French War the capture and pillage of the settlement by a Jacobin squadron—no description can be given here. Suffice it to say that the man whose courage and capacity saved the situation was Zachary Macaulay. Sent out in 1793 as a member of the Council, he succeeded to the Governorship in the following year, when he was only twenty-six; and, when he retired in 1799, he had nursed the infant settlement through its worst phase and left it so well-established that in 1807, the pioneer work having been done and the experiment justified, the British Government was prepared to take it over as a Crown Colony.

Such was the " positive policy " of the Abolitionists, a policy woven from its earliest conception of three distinct but interrelated threads —Christianity, commerce, colonization.

n.b.

work of the clapham Act inspired african association 1788 "for the discovery of the Interior parts of africa". Commissioned Mungo Park for his journey in 1795

1792 - Baptist Missionary Soc.
1798 - London Missionary Soc.
1799 - Church Missionary Soc.
1803 - British & Foreign Bible Soc.
1818 Wesleyan Methodist Missionary Society.

CHAPTER IV

THE ABOLITION OF THE BRITISH SLAVE TRADE

THE campaign against the Slave Trade may be said to have begun when in the autumn of 1787 Clarkson set out on the first of his many journeys of investigation. He visited Bristol, Liverpool, and Lancaster. He boarded slave-ships and measured the quarters provided for slaves. He checked the muster-rolls to establish the high proportion of deaths among the British crews. He obtained specimens of the shackles, thumbscrews and mouth-openers in use. He asked questions of everyone concerned. And naturally he provoked resentment and hostility : for though no one imagined that this busybody's curiosity could conceivably be dangerous to so great and old an institution as the Trade, it might be dangerous to individual traders. Many things were done on slave-ships which were best kept dark. Once, indeed, Clarkson got on the track of the murder of a seaman by his captain. Some of the Liverpool traders, therefore, began to follow and molest him and try to force a quarrel on him, and one day they nearly succeeded in hustling him into a high sea off the pier-head. But Clarkson never lacked courage.

He completed his inquiries and returned to London loaded with deadly evidence.

Throughout this autumn and winter Wilberforce was also hard at work, preparing himself for the part he was to play in Parliament. He read all he could find about the Trade. He talked to London business-men concerned in it. He discussed it with his political friends and especially with Pitt. There was plenty else to occupy the young Prime Minister's mind—the state of the King's health, the Hastings case, the trouble in the Low Countries, the Russian attack on Turkey—but, when he recommended Wilberforce to take up the cause of Abolition, he did not mean to wash his hands of it himself. Indeed he hated the Trade as much as Wilberforce hated it ; but, as he frankly explained to him at the outset and as Wilberforce fully understood, he could not make Abolition a Government measure for the simple reason that his Government was not agreed on it. Thurlow, for instance, the Lord Chancellor, and Sydney, the Secretary of State concerned with colonial questions, were stubbornly opposed to any tampering with the Trade. But, short of committing his Government or his party, Pitt was prepared to do all he could for the cause. He gave many hours of his time to Wilberforce. He interviewed Clarkson at his suggestion and listened to his evidence. And he took two active steps. In order to provide authoritative material for opening the attack in Parliament, he instructed the Trade Committee of the Privy Council to inquire into and report on British trade with Africa; and with a view to undermining the case against a one-sided Abolition on Britain's part he told the British Ambassador in Paris to sound the French Government as to the possibility of joint action; if France were sympathetic, similar approaches were to be made to Spain and Holland. The Privy Council Report was duly presented in the spring of 1789 and admirably served its purpose. But the diplomatic move led nowhere. The French Minister refused to commit himself; and, if France stood out, it seemed useless to raise the issue with other nations. Pitt, nevertheless, was now determined on British Abolition, however one-sided and however profitable to less conscientious rivals. "Called at Pitt's to-night," Wilberforce noted in his diary early in 1788; "he firm about African trade, though we begin to perceive more difficulties in the way than we had hoped there would be."

It had been decided to open the battle in the House of Commons in the course of 1788, but in March Wilberforce, whose health was never strong, fell so desperately ill—his doctors practically gave him up—that Pitt promised him, "with a warmth of principle and friendship that has made me love him better than I ever did before," to assume himself the leadership of the attack in Parliament, and, after a conference with Sharp, he moved on May 9 a resolution binding the House to consider the Slave Trade early in the next session when the Privy Council Committee, over which he was now presiding in person, would have reported. He deprecated discussion at that stage and reserved his own opinion. Fox and Burke, on the other hand, both declared themselves outright for Abolition. The supporters of the Trade, reserving their defence, said little. The resolution was carried *nem. con.* It was a brief and rather formal debate, but in itself it marked a notable change from the mute acquiescence of the Commons in North's pessimism in 1783. And more was done before the session closed. Sir William Dolben, member for Oxford University, visited a slave-ship lying in the Thames and was so horrified at the arrangements for the tight packing of its human cargo that he at once gave notice of a Bill to limit for the time being the number of slaves to be carried in proportion to a ship's tonnage. This brought the Trade's supporters into the open. They not only denied the slaves' sufferings ; they declared that any attempt to regulate the Trade would ruin it. On both counts they made a tactical mistake. Their attempt to minimize the hardships of the " Middle Passage " made little impression on the House beside the fact, now admitted, that sometimes one-third of the slaves died in the course of it ; and their intransigence provoked Pitt to vigorous action. He told the Commons, that, if indeed the Trade were incapable of regulation, then he would vote without further inquiry for its entire abolition—a declaration which ensured the passage of the Bill by an overwhelming majority —and when it was threatened with destruction in the Lords, he saved it by the narrow margin of two votes by letting it be known that, if it were lost, he would not remain in the same Cabinet as its opponents.

In April, 1789, the Privy Council Report was published. It stated no opinion on the Trade, but it printed the evidence taken on it ; and, though the solid arguments for maintaining the Trade were fully stated on the one side, together with a good deal of less substantial " whitewash," a long series of respectable witnesses on the other side—colonial administrators, naval officers, doctors, travellers—had given evidence of the actual operation of the Trade as they themselves had seen it. Clarkson had reported the results of his inquiries and had introduced some of his informants from the slave-ports. Particularly telling, because so obviously disinterested, was the evidence of Dr. Andrew Sparrman, professor of Physics at Stockholm and a well-known African traveller, who described how a drunken native " king," desiring to buy more brandy, sent out his warriors to make a night-raid on a neighbouring village for slaves. The net result was damning. " The more we consider the case," wrote Pitt after discussing the Report with Speaker Grenville, " the more irresistible it is in all its parts ; "

and it was not without hope of success that on May 12 Wilberforce, who had astonished the doctors by a quick and complete recovery from his illness, rose to move a series of resolutions concerted with Pitt, which summarized the case against the Trade. For over three hours he held the attention of the House with a speech which no less a master than Burke declared to be comparable with " the remains of Grecian eloquence." He was followed by Burke who argued that the commerce lost by Abolition would not be enough to justify the old plea of " necessity," and in any case, " are we not prepared," he asked, " to pay the price of virtue : " by Pitt who, as everyone had foretold since the debates on Dolben's Bill, ranked himself unequivocally with Wilberforce : and by Fox who refused to believe that France would block the way to Abolition, she might be expected, rather, " to catch a spark from the light of our fire and run a race with us in promoting the ends of humanity." The speeches on the other side were poor. No one on the front benches defended the Trade. It was left to " West Indians " and " back-benchers." And yet, though argument and authority seemed all on one side, the House as a whole was not yet ready to make up its mind. Conscience was in conflict with native caution. " Men distinguished for philanthropy," said Sir Guy Cooper, " might be hurried to the adoption of a measure which tended to the injury of our West India islands. He confessed he entertained much doubt and perplexity on the subject." The general feeling could not have been better stated ; and, when it was adroitly suggested that the Commons ought not to determine the issue without hearing the evidence at its own Bar, the House jumped at this chance of evading an immediate choice, and despite Pitt's and Fox's protests voted to have all the evidence recited over again. It was an honest, a characteristic decision. It meant delay, but nothing more favourable to the " West Indian " cause than that.

No further progress was made in 1790. Evidence was heard all through the session, and at the close of it there was a General Election which strengthened Pitt's majority. But the Abolitionists did not waste the time. Clarkson was busy in the provinces, creating local centres of Abolitionist opinion, and Wilberforce was studying the Privy Council Report and such new evidence as was given in the Commons. " Continued to work very hard at the evidence all this week. Slept ill, partly through working too much "—such entries constantly recur in Wilberforce's diary of that year. When, therefore, in the spring of 1791, he moved for " leave to bring in a Bill to prevent the further importation of slaves into the British islands in the West Indies," his speech, while as eloquent and moderate in tone as its predecessor, was more closely packed with facts and illustrations. Again Pitt, Fox and Burke supported Wilberforce. Again, though this time the Trade had some more respectable backers such as Sir William Yonge and Lord John Russell, no leading politician defended it.

> The leaders, it is true [said Mr. Drake], are for Abolition. But the minor orators, the dwarfs, the pygmies will, I trust, this day carry the question against them. The property of the West Indians is at stake ; and, though men may be generous with their own property, they should not be so with the property of others.

It was a misinterpretation of the letter of Wilberforce's motion, but not of its spirit. Slavery itself would be in danger if the Trade were destroyed. And now that the House could no longer postpone its decision, it allowed the appeals which Fox had made to its humanity and Pitt to its sense of justice to be muffled by its traditional dislike of drastic change and its traditional respect for the rights of property. The motion was rejected by 163 votes to 88.

The Abolitionists, of course, did not accept this parliamentary verdict. They at once determined to work for its reversal by the only practicable means—by mobilizing public opinion against it. The propaganda organized by the Committee was already bearing fruit. Pamphlets on the horrors of the Trade and reprints of the debates in Parliament had been widely distributed. A poem by Cowper, *The Negro's Complaint*, had been set to music and thousands of copies of it circulated. A cameo depicting a Negro in an attitude of entreaty had been designed by Wedgwood, the famous master-potter and an ardent Abolitionist, and widely adopted for decorating snuff-boxes, bracelets and hairpins. A campaign had been launched, not unsuccessfully, to encourage the consumption of East Indian sugar instead of the slave-grown West Indian product. And the outcome of all this had been a great increase in the number of English men and women who knew the black facts of the Trade and wanted to stop it. All that was needed, therefore, was to canalize this current of public opinion and bring it to bear in full volume upon Parliament. Early in 1792, therefore, a systematic plan of action was put in operation. A new abstract of the case against the Trade was broadcasted together with a summary of the last debate. On its heels Clarkson set out on another exhaustive tour through England while Dr. Dickson was dispatched to Scotland. Corresponding Committees were set up all over the country in liaison with the London Committee, and under their guidance petitions against the Trade were prepared to await the day when Wilberforce should again give notice of an Abolition motion in the Commons. This machinery went like clockwork. The notice of motion was given early in 1792. Instantly the petitions began to pour in—312 from England, 187 from Scotland. Only five were presented from the other side—even Liverpool abstaining.

In the City, the Lord Mayor and a majority of the Aldermen opposed a petition from the Common Council, but the Liverymen defied them and their petition reached the House on April 2, 1792, just as Wilberforce rose to open the greatest parliamentary battle ever fought on the issue of the slave-system.

The opposition had not been idle ; and, as it happened, the course of events abroad had given them a more powerful weapon than any they had hitherto possessed. Already at the time of the debate in the previous year the storm was gathering across the Channel which was presently to sweep the world. During 1791 the French Revolution began to drift into its more violent and aggressive phase. By the end of the year an armed conflict between the new France it had brought to birth and the forces of the *ancien régime* in Europe had become inevitable. In 1792, in terrible *crescendo*, came the singing of the *Marseillaise*, the declaration of war on Prussia, the imprisonment of the King, the " September Massacres," and the invasion of Belgium. The reaction of these events on English opinion was profound. The attitude of most Englishmen which had been tolerant if not sympathetic towards the Revolution in its earlier and more constitutional stage changed to hate and fear. The tide of toleration which had been flowing since 1783 abruptly turned. Progressive policies were at a discount. Reform was shelved for forty years. And the anti-

Slavery movement which was grounded on the ideas of natural rights and liberties—the very ideas which had kindled the flames in France—inevitably suffered with the rest. Unhappily, moreover, a concrete example of the risks inherent in tampering with the established order of society in the West Indies was provided by the effects of the Revolution in the French islands and especially the French section of Haiti or St. Domingue. In the course of 1791 that populous and fertile colony was plunged into anarchy and bloodshed. First the French Royalists fought the French Republicans : then the mulattoes rose, demanding equality with the whites ; and finally the slaves, some 100,000 strong, let loose the horrors of a " servile war." About 2,000 whites were massacred. Over 1,000 plantations were destroyed. And inevitably the infection spread. The slaves of other French islands rose. There was even an abortive rising in the little British island of Dominica. And the moral of it all from the viewpoint of the " West Indians " was obvious. " Look what comes of undermining the old and natural subordination of blacks to whites with Jacobin ideas."

It was difficult for members of the House to shut their eyes to those red danger-signals from Paris and St. Domingue : but it was equally difficult to disregard the unprecedented demonstration of public opinion embodied in the petitions, backed as it was by their own conviction that the atrocities committed by the Trade in Africa and in the " Middle Passage " could no longer be disputed. When, therefore, a compromise was again suggested, again they jumped at it. The lead was given by Dundas, Pitt's closest colleague in the Cabinet and the shrewdest of his party-managers. He supported Abolition, but it should be *gradual* Abolition : and the best method of bringing it about was to better the condition of the slaves, to encourage their breeding, and to educate their children, so that the planters, finding themselves supplied with a labour-force, adequate in number and improved in quality, would no longer need the Trade, and the way would be open for a transition from slave-labour to free. As Parliament was to realize some thirty years later, the enforcement of such ameliorating regulations was impracticable : the planters would have none of them. But at the time it seemed a reasonable compromise. Dundas, indeed, had taken a leaf out of the Abolitionists' book. His plan was akin to Burke's plan of 1780, and Burke, influenced perhaps on this issue as on others by his growing horror of the Revolution, had sent Dundas a copy of his draft code of regulations, but he took no part in the debate. Wilberforce and his allies, on the other hand, could not be expected to accept the proposal. It permitted the Trade to continue its evil work day after day, year after year. It gave no certain assurance that it would ever stop. So, while

Speaker Addington and Jenkinson, afterwards
Lord Liverpool, responded to Dundas' appeal
for the formation of a group of " moderates " to
" reduce the question to its proper bounds,"
Fox vigorously denounced a policy of " moderation " in murder and rapine and appealed for
the honest course of immediate and total Abolition. " As long as I have a voice to speak,
this question shall never be at rest." All
through the night the debate dragged on and
dawn was nearly breaking when Pitt rose to
wind it up. Troubled by the division on the
question in his Cabinet and his party and recognizing the damaging effects of the tragedy in
St. Domingue, he had disquieted Wilberforce
by suggesting a postponement of the debate ;
and indeed in Whig or Radical circles his loyalty
to the cause of Abolition was now seriously

Pitts Speech.

questioned. All such doubts were dispelled by
his speech. It was probably the finest in his
career. Fox, Grey and Windham agreed that
" it was one of the most extraordinary displays
of eloquence they had ever heard." He directly
met the panic-mongers by arguing that, if indeed
the British islands were threatened with the fate
of St. Domingue, obviously no more slaves
should be imported. In answer to Dundas and
his " moderates " he urged that immediate Abolition would compel the planters to adopt in
their own interests the suggested programme of
amelioration. Above all he pleaded that atonement for " our long and cruel injustice towards

Africa " should not be delayed for one more hour. Let no one say that " Providence has inexorably doomed her to be only a nursery of slaves for us free and civilized Europeans." The abolition of the Trade would open a new era in her life—and, as he reached this peroration, the rising sun began to shine through the windows of the House—it would usher in the dawn of civilization in Africa. . . . A great speech, but the House had made up its mind to follow the " moderates." The votes cast for Wilberforce's motion numbered 125, those for Dundas' amendment 193. The motion as amended, " That the Slave Trade ought to be gradually abolished," was carried by 230 to 85.

The Abolitionists were not unduly discouraged by this debate. To have secured, after only a few years of agitation, an overwhelming majority of the Commons for gradual Abolition was a remarkable achievement ; and it was soon clear that most of the " moderates " sincerely desired the gradual process to be brief. Dundas himself was willing to fix the date for the termination of the Trade at 1800, and after some haggling it was fixed as early as 1796 by 151 votes to 132. But the most formidable of all the obstacles to Abolition was still to be overcome. The House of Lords was less amenable to the pressure of public opinion than the lower chamber. It was presided over by Lord Chancellor Thurlow, the Trade's best friend in the Cabinet and Pitt's worst enemy, and it represented in Rodney the antagonism of the Navy to Abolition and in the Duke of Clarence and his brothers the antipathy of the Court. All Grenville's weight and earnestness, therefore, could not prevent the Lords from adopting, with less excuse than the Commons, the obstructive device of hearing the evidence again. By the end of the session they had found time to hear only seven witnesses; and, before the slow process was resumed, almost all the ground which the Abolitionists had gained, both inside and outside Parliament, had been cut away by the outbreak of war with France.

The war unquestionably strengthened the material case against Abolition. Was it not more than ever foolish now to endanger the stability of the British West Indies, to weaken the mercantile marine, to diminish the commercial profits of the nation? Ought we not, rather, to use our sea-power to capture the French West Indian islands and the French share of the Trade? But the effect of the war on public opinion went deeper than that. All Europe, it seemed, was now threatened by the authors of the Terror. Reaction stiffened. Even liberal-minded Englishmen were inclined for the most part to postpone consideration of reforms till the danger was over. And in the atmosphere of war it was easier to credit the suggestion that any Englishman who played with such Revolutionary fire as Abolition was no true patriot. Already before the war Clarkson had betrayed a dangerous sympathy with the Revolution at a little public meeting in London : and, when Wilberforce's conscience forced him to adopt a less bellicose tone than the Government and to make the most of any possibilities of peace, the champions of the Trade triumphantly asserted that all Abolitionists were Jacobins at heart. And if among Wilberforce's political friends there were none who questioned his patriotism, there were many who questioned his wisdom in not leaving the Trade alone for the duration of the war. It seemed, after all, a common-sense policy, and it was apparently what the country wanted. The Abolitionist enthusiasm of 1792 faded quickly away in 1793. It was reported from several centres that no further collective action was practicable, that nobody except " Republicans " would sign another petition. Once more in the winter of 1793 Clarkson set out on a pilgrimage of propaganda, but he found public opinion more interested now in fighting Frenchmen than slave-traders, and his nervous system, strained to the limit by his exertions of the past few years, completely broke down. And then even the stalwarts of the Abolition Committee began to waver. It only met occasionally in 1794, only twice in 1795 and in 1796, and then it ceased to meet at all till 1804.

But, hopeless as it now might seem, Wilberforce refused to suspend the attack upon the Trade. He was abused and ridiculed. Calumnies were spread abroad about his private life.

He was twice challenged by slave-captains to fight a duel. But he held to his course. From the outset he had conceived the fight for Abolition as a sacred duty, as a crusade ; and in his eyes the war made it not less but more urgent for a nation that put its trust in God to cease from sinning. When he was asked if the report was true that he was " about to give up the cause of the poor African until a quieter season," he replied that it was impossible. " When the actual commission of guilt is in question, a man who fears God is not at liberty." So, session after session, he continued to move his Abolition resolution, and, session after session, it was rejected. In vain he reminded the Commons of what they had resolved should happen in 1796 : the year came and passed and nothing was done. He carried a Bill for prohibiting slave-trading with foreign countries through the Commons, but it was thrown out by the Lords. A similar Bill to restrict the Trade to a section of the African coast suffered the same fate. Only two minor steps were taken on the slaves' behalf in all the first ten years of the war. An Act was passed to widen the space between decks on slave-ships and to reward masters and surgeons for a low death-rate on the voyage, and an address was carried asking that colonial Governors should recommend their legislatures to ameliorate the conditions of Slavery. This last move provoked a sharp rejoinder from Jamaica. While not unwilling to consider measures of amelioration, the Assembly refused to regard them as in any way conducive to the ultimate cessation of the Trade and protested vigorously against interference by the Imperial Parliament in their domestic concerns. But Parliament was no longer contemplating any drastic interference. It was back at the stage when the Trade, and still more Slavery itself, were regarded as painful " necessities " which might indeed be " ameliorated " but could not be abolished. In 1799 Wilberforce confessed to the House that his cause seemed weaker now than when he had first espoused it in 1787.

Throughout that gloomy period Wilberforce was almost without allies. Burke's closing years —he died in 1797—were obsessed by his hatred of Jacobinism. Fox and his little group of Radicals deserted the House of Commons from 1797 to 1801 in futile protest against the dominant reaction. Of other leading politicians Windham changed over from the Abolitionist to the " West Indian " side, but Canning, whose mordant eloquence was beginning to command attention, came out for Abolition. Dundas, from the moment the war broke out, set his face against any further discussion of the Trade. He bluntly told Wilberforce in 1794 that he would use all his influence with Pitt and his other colleagues in the Government " to prevent any question on the subject being agitated, at least during the war." But Pitt—and this compensated for a host of defections—remained stubbornly loyal to Wilberforce. As the war continued on its long and disappointing course, as the conflict with the Revolution developed into a fight for national freedom with Napoleon, the burden of his office began to wear down his strength; and he would doubtless have been not a little relieved if he could have persuaded Wilberforce to agree with Dundas and suspend his crusade till peace-time. But, Wilberforce persisting, he seems to have felt himself bound in honour to support him. He never again made so great a speech on Abolition as that of 1792; but, when Wilberforce, year after year, forced the question on the House, Pitt always spoke as well as voted on his side.

By 1800 the fortunes of the cause had sunk to their lowest. In 1801 Pitt resigned on the Irish issue and was succeeded by Addington, whose " moderation " in 1792 had stiffened into firm antagonism to Abolition. The Peace of Amiens (1802–3), which inspired in Wilberforce a fleeting hope that the negotiating Powers might be persuaded to consider a universal abolition of the Trade, only served to convince the British people that the war was bound to go on till they or Napoleon had been finally defeated. So dark now was the prospect that Wilberforce himself was at last persuaded that the preaching of his cause could do no good. In 1800 and for the next three years he did not move his usual resolution. So little did he suspect that at this very time the tide at last was on the turn. If his pertinacity in keeping the question before Parliament had done nothing else, it had at least reminded the public, year in, year out, of the harsh facts of the case, and all the time, beneath the surface of " war-mentality " and reaction, the old philanthropic instincts had been quietly recovering their hold. Men of influence outside politics were making their opinions felt—men like Dr. Porteous, the Evangelical Archbishop of Canterbury, or Jeremy Bentham, father of the Utilitarian movement. The war, too, was no longer quite the obstacle it was. After ten years Englishmen were becoming, so to speak, accustomed to it and less inclined to accept its veto on every measure not concerned with its prosecution. Nor could suspicions of Jacobinism, since Napoleon had killed it, be used any longer to discredit the Abolitionist cause. And, finally, the ranks of its most interested opponents had begun to split. British operations in the Caribbean had resulted, at a disproportionate cost of life, in the acquisition of sundry French and Dutch colonies, the soil of which, particularly the Dutch, was exceptionally fertile and had not yet been widely used for cultivating sugar. To a growing section of " West Indians " it seemed likely that the development of these new sugar-fields would still further depress the declining fortunes of the older British islands, and, since that development could only be prevented by stopping the supply of African labour, they began to reconsider their intransigent rejection of Abolition and to contemplate at least the suspension of the Trade for a period of years.

Thus in 1804 the way had unexpectedly opened for a renewal of the campaign. Once more the Abolition Committee met, strengthened by such valuable new members as Stephen, Macaulay, and Brougham. Once more, on May 30, Wilberforce repeated his old motion for leave to introduce an Abolition Bill. Pitt, again Prime Minister, supported it as of old. So did Fox, now back in the House. And many of the new Irish members, brought to Westminster by the Act of Union, were ready to vote for a measure which did no injury to Irish interests. The outcome was a clean swing-back to 1792. Though opposed by Castlereagh and Windham and most but not all of the "West Indians," the Bill was duly introduced, and passed its second reading by 100 votes to 42 and its third by 69 to 33. It was launched at once in the Lords, but, as the session was near its end, a division on it was put off till the following year. Wilberforce and his allies could reconcile themselves to this delay with victory at last so near at hand, but they had still to suffer the bitterest of all their many disappointments. Prevented by the King's antagonism to Fox from forming a national coalition, forced to bear almost single-handed and in failing health the double burden of fighting Napoleon in Europe and a vigorous Opposition at Westminster, Pitt was more disinclined than he had ever been to spend strength and provoke controversy on the side-issue of Abolition. The admission of Addington into his Cabinet made it still more difficult. Early in 1805, therefore, he asked Wilberforce to postpone for a time the reintroduction of his Bill. But Wilberforce, devoted though he had been all his life to Pitt, refused to make his " holy cause subservient to the interests of a party," and the Bill was reintroduced. On the second reading Pitt spoke only to rebut an incidental charge against his Government : for the first time he said nothing in support of Abolition. His silence probably made little difference ; his opinion was notorious ; and what mainly determined the result, no doubt, was the last desperate effort of the Trade to whip up its supporters and the unexpected defection of the Irish members. The second reading was refused by 77 votes to 70. Only one minor success could be recorded in what was to have been the year of victory. After many months of procrastination, Pitt's promise to Wilberforce to prevent by a proclamation or Order-in-Council the stocking of the annexed colonies with new slaves was fulfilled at last in September.

It has been said that Pitt was the main obstacle to the earlier achievement of Abolition. If this is true at all, if the delay was due to Pitt rather than to circumstances he could not override, it is only true of the last year of his life, when his strength was failing under the crushing burden of the war. In January, 1806, he died ; and in the coalition under Grenville which thereupon came into power Fox obtained again the office he had not held since 1783. His health also was failing—he died before the year's end—but in the few months left him he was determined to kill the Slave Trade. It was still impossible to make Abolition a Government measure with Windham and Addington, now Lord Sidmouth, in the Cabinet; but a majority of Ministers, including their chief, were in favour of it, and they had behind them a revival of public feeling. In the previous winter Clarkson, emerging from his long retirement, had made another of his tours and reported that a new generation of Abolitionists had grown up as ardent in the cause as the old one of pre-war days. The prospects seemed still more favourable when a Foreign Slave Trade Bill, replacing the Order-in-Council and extending its prohibition to foreign colonies, was introduced as a preliminary trial of strength and passed both Houses. There could thus be little doubt of the result when on June 10 Fox moved his resolution in the familiar terms of Wilberforce's resolutions in the past. " If," he said of the enactment of Abolition, " during the almost forty years that I have now had the honour of a seat in Parliament, I had been so fortunate as to accomplish that and that only, I should think I had done enough and could retire from public life with comfort and the conscious satisfaction that I had done my duty." The motion was carried by the great majority of

Despite all his faults
C.J. Fox ended his career
in glory.

114 to 15. Introduced by Grenville in the Lords, it was carried there also by 41 to 30. It was evident that next year would see the end— so evident that, to prevent attempts at forestalling, a Bill was rushed through both Houses before the session closed to prohibit the employment in the Trade of any ships not hitherto employed therein.

The dissolution of Parliament and a General Election in the autumn maintained the Government in office, and it was decided that the Abolition Bill should be the first and principal measure of the new session and should be started on its course in the Lords. On January 2, 1807, accordingly, it was introduced by Grenville. The first clause of the Bill as finally enacted prescribed that after January 1, 1808, " all manner of dealing and trading " in slaves in Africa or in their transport from Africa to any other place was to be " utterly abolished, prohibited and declared to be unlawful," and that any British subject acting to the contrary would be fined £100 for every slave so purchased, sold or transported. The second clause declared that any British ship engaged in the Trade would be forfeited to the Crown. Other clauses provided for the penalization of insurance-contracts made on the Trade's behalf, for the payment of bounties to naval officers and men for the recovery of slaves from ships violating the Act, and for putting such rescued slaves at the disposal of the Crown. On the second reading on February 5,

the Bill was vigorously attacked by the Duke
of Clarence, Jenkinson (now Lord Hawkesbury),
Eldon, and St. Vincent who walked out of the
House in angry protest, but it was supported by
the Duke of Gloucester, the Bishop of Durham
and seven other peers, and carried by 100 votes
to 36. On February 23 the second reading was
moved in the Commons. The House was fairly
full and evidently determined to pass the Bill.
The few speeches made against it were heard in
silence. Such leading opponents as Windham
and Castlereagh did not speak at all. The climax
of the debate was reached when a daring contrast drawn by Solicitor-General Romilly between Napoleon and Wilberforce brought the
House to its feet in a storm of cheering for the
man whose indomitable perseverance was now
at last to be rewarded. The vote was overwhelming—283 to 16. The Bill was read a third
time on March 16, returned to the Lords on
March 23, and received the King's assent on
March 25.

The Act of 1807, which became operative on
January 1, 1808, was promptly enforced by
British cruisers, and the great majority of British
" slavers " were quickly driven from the seas.
But so great were the profits of the Trade that
a few brazen speculators were still to be found
in Britain prepared to violate the law and to
risk one or two captures and the serious financial
penalties the Act imposed, if only they could
smuggle one cargo safely through. Groups were

formed to fit out slave-ships at continental ports and even at Liverpool and London. In 1811, therefore, an amending Act was passed making Slave Trading a felony punishable with transportation. That proved effective; the hardiest gambler shrank from the horrors of Van Dieman's Land or Botany Bay. And the further Act of 1824, making the Trade piracy and a capital crime, which was passed mainly as a matter of principle and as an example to other nations, was found to be unnecessary and repealed in 1837.

The British Slave Trade may be said to have been doomed when Sharp, Clarkson, Wilberforce and their little band of propagandists opened their countrymen's eyes to the actual brutalities it involved, when such men of light and leading as Wesley, Adam Smith, Porteous, and Bentham came out against it, and when the House of Commons, headed by Pitt and Fox and Burke, was converted to the principle of Abolition. It is not surprising that the Revolution and the war delayed its achievement. More remarkable, indeed, is the fact that, only twenty years after the campaign had started, while the war was still continuing and at a critical phase, a commercial organization, so great and old-established, so immensely profitable, buttressed by such powerful vested interests and regarded so recently as a permanent, if regrettable, necessity of European civilization, should have been destroyed.

" The conscience of the British people awakened and a humanitarian tradition planted in the heart of British politics (Coupland CH.III., II - V.)

CHAPTER V

THE ABOLITION OF SLAVERY IN THE
BRITISH COLONIES

THE abolition of the Slave Trade was in itself a great achievement, but it had always been regarded by its promoters as a means to a greater end. "The emancipation of the slaves," said Wilberforce in 1823, "was the ultimate object of all those who took the lead as advocates for the abolition of the Slave Trade," and on another occasion he cited Pitt, Fox, Grenville, and Grey as believing that, once the Trade was abolished, Slavery itself would steadily diminish and finally disappear. It was expected that the planters, deprived of fresh supplies of slaves from Africa, would be forced to treat better those they already possessed in order to extend their length of life and service and to promote their natural increase. Overwork and cruel punishments would be avoided. Marriage would be encouraged. To prevent the rupture of family-life slaves would tend to be tied to the soil and so to advance from slavery to serfdom. And finally, as the conditions of their life improved and they became more and more civilized, the transition to full freedom would be smoothly and equitably accomplished.

Such hopes would not have been unreasonable if the planters had been amenable to reason. But the planters for the most part were now in an angry and obstinate mood. Though the Abolitionists had refrained as a general rule from directly attacking Slavery, criticism of its methods had proved inseparable from the attack on the Trade ; and the slave-owners had bitterly resented such criticism, the more bitterly the more truth there was in it. Not all of them were so ferocious as Mr. Molyneux whose calumnious assault on Ramsay's character in the House of Commons was thought to have hastened the latter's death and who wrote to his natural son in St. Christopher, " Ramsay is dead : I have killed him." But as a body the planters hated the humanitarian leaders—hated them so hotly that they lost sight of the evident fact that Wilberforce and his allies had behind them the great body of British public opinion. And that blindness led them into a suicidal mistake. If they had recognized that they were now dealing not with the whims of a few pious fanatics—as they chose to regard the Abolitionists—but with the sober good-nature of the British people, if they had pocketed their pride and coolly consulted their own interests, if they had set themselves genuinely to improve the lot of their slaves, the end of Slavery might have been long postponed. But they did none of these things. They stiffened their necks. They denied the right of any body in England, of Parliament itself, to interfere in their domestic concerns. They would do what they liked with their own property. To accept suggestions, however gentle, of " amelioration " would be a confession of guilt and an admission that those detestable busybodies knew better how slaves should be treated than they did themselves. The planters' policy, in fact, was one of flat defiance ; and in adopting it they lost their chance of successfully appealing to the inherent caution and fair-mindedness of British public opinion and of playing on its love of compromise and dislike of violent courses. If they had been wiser, the abolition of Slavery would have been none the less sure in the end, but, as the Abolitionists themselves expected, it would have been slow. The planters' conduct made it sure and swift.

Already before the Napoleonic War was ended, reports from the West Indies had made it clear that the effective abolition of the British Slave Trade by the Acts of 1807 and 1811 and the vigilance of the British Navy in enforcing them had not induced the planters to mend their ways. In 1815, accordingly, the Abolitionists took two steps. An address to the Crown was voted by both Houses of Parliament asking that the Colonial Assemblies should be strongly recommended to promote the physical, moral and religious improvement of the slaves. That meant, said Canning in a speech intended for the planters' ears, " You are safe for the present from the interference of the British Parliament in the belief that, left to yourselves, you will do what is required of you." But they did not do it. Only one or two of the colonial legislatures inserted some minor improvements in their "slave-codes," and nobody in the islands seems to have supposed that such laws were meant to be kept. Secondly, Wilberforce introduced a Bill to prevent the illicit importation of new slaves by the compulsory registration of all slaves—a simple and efficacious device which had been conceived by James Stephen and applied in 1812 to Trinidad and later to St. Lucia, which, together with Demerara and Berbice (afterwards united as British Guiana), were Crown Colonies without Legislative Assemblies such as the other colonies possessed, and subject therefore to legislation by Orders-in-Council from Downing Street. The Bill was fiercely opposed by the "West Indians," who denied that any smuggling had occurred and denounced the measure as a wanton violation of their liberties; and Castlereagh persuaded the Commons to allow the colonial legislatures to establish registers themselves. On this occasion they took the hint. Only Tobago and Grenada, however, adopted the efficient Trinidad system: the other islands omitted to make the sale of unregistered slaves illegal—an essential provision—and some of them, notably Jamaica, made little effort to complete or enforce the registration. In 1819, accordingly, the British Parliament put on the screw by enacting that duplicates of the registers should be lodged in London and that the sale or mortgage in England of any slave not entered therein should be invalid.

Meantime the renewal of discussion on the slave-system had reproduced the hectic atmosphere which had enveloped the first attack upon the Trade. Though Wilberforce's prestige among his countrymen was now as high and safe in its way as Wellington's, all the old slanderous abuse was heaped on him again in the colonial press ; and, as in earlier years, this violent talk excited and provoked the slaves. From island to island the rumour spread that their masters were withholding the freedom which Parliament had already granted. In Barbados they rose and did considerable damage to sugar-canes and buildings on some sixty estates, but no white man was killed. The troops easily suppressed the rising : several hundred slaves were killed in action : and many of the prisoners were tried and executed. See what happens, said the planters as they had said before, when those incorrigible meddlers in England play with fire.

Wilberforce, of course, was not deterred by these attacks. On the contrary, observing the way in which history was repeating itself, he began to think that with Slavery as with the Trade " amelioration " would prove impracticable and Abolition was the only remedy. At the beginning of 1818 the idea of pressing for clean " emancipation " first figures in his private journal. And, if for the moment he refrained

116

from raising the issue directly, mainly because public opinion was preoccupied with the post-war problems of destitution and unrest at home, he determined to prepare the ground for a direct attack by drawing the attention of Parliament and thereby of the Press and the public to the steadily accumulating evidence of the cruelties which " unameliorated " Slavery inflicted on its victims. Motions were made by him and by his old friend and ally, Romilly, for papers on the treatment of the slaves ; and in making them they cited from official records some terrible cases of murderous maltreatment and of the failure of the local courts to punish it. " As to those laws which look so well on paper," said Romilly, echoing Burke's criticism of the slave-codes, " they not only are not executed, but were never intended to be executed ; " and he quoted Governor Prevost's opinion that the sole purpose of an ameliorating Act recently passed in Dominica was " to prevent the interference of the mother country in the management of the slaves." These opening moves were well conceived and did their work. Parliament was in a humanitarian mood. It was legislating about that time to soften the barbarous rigour of the criminal code, to save pickpockets from the gallows, to regulate the employment of children in industry, to prevent cruelty to animals ; and in such an atmosphere the facts about Slavery were bound to tell at least as much as the facts about the Slave Trade had told thirty years before. It seemed undeniable that many slaves were ill-treated. Could it also be denied that their only hope of protection lay in Parliament ?

Before that crucial question was faced and answered, Wilberforce had resigned the parliamentary leadership of the campaign. Never robust, his health had been increasingly affected by the long hours and bad air of the House of Commons ; and in 1821, after consulting Stephen and others of his closest colleagues, he wrote to Thomas Fowell Buxton, who had recently proved himself to be one of the most effective speakers among the younger members of the House, and invited him to assume the rôle of political spearhead to the anti-Slavery movement.

Physically no two men could have been more unlike—Wilberforce, the "Shrimp," small, slender, frail and stooping, "Elephant Buxton," as his schoolfellows called him, holding erect an unusually tall and massive figure. Nor had Buxton Wilberforce's silver voice or easy eloquence or quick subtlety of mind. His strength in politics was primarily strength of character. The fruit of unsparing labour and hard thought, his speeches were as massive as his frame. Wilberforce likened his work in the House to " hewing statues out of rock," and Sir James Mackintosh described one speech he made as " the most powerful appeal " he had ever heard in it. But in their attitude to life, in their sense of public duty, and above all in their deep religious faith, veteran and recruit were close akin. Buxton, like Wilberforce, lost his father when he was only a few years old, and it was from his mother, a Quakeress, that he early acquired that unsleeping sense of the seriousness of life which haunted him to the end. "He never was a child," said a friend in later days. His intimacy with the Quaker community in Norfolk which centred round the Gurney family at Earlham, his marriage with Hannah Gurney, his friendship with his wife's sister, Elizabeth Fry, and his brother-in-law, Samuel Hoare—all these personal associations confirmed and strengthened his religious convictions and his earnestness of purpose. But, like Wilberforce again, he was neither prig nor pietist. He thoroughly enjoyed life, especially the life of a country squire. He loved dogs and horses and was devoted to all field-sports. But more and more as time went on the demands of public service drew him from the fields to London. In 1818, at the age of 32, having decided that Parliament was "the sphere in which I could do most for my Master's service," he was elected for Weymouth and threw himself at once into the battle for reforming the prisons and the penal code. It was his success therein which determined Wilberforce, who had made his acquaintance through the Gurneys, to offer him the leadership of the anti-Slavery crusade. Taught by his mother to abominate Slavery, surrounded since boyhood by humanitarian influences, Buxton had supported the Abolitionist

cause almost as a matter of course ; but feeling
that its conduct in Parliament was safe in Wilberforce's hands, he had hitherto directed his
energy and industry elsewhere ; and when the
call came to accept the prophetic mantle from
the man whom he and all his friends regarded
as the best and greatest man in public life, he
was too uncertain of his own powers, too cautious
in judgment and thorough in method, to respond
at once. He set himself first to master the subject. For more than a year he gave all his spare
time to the study of books and pamphlets and
reports on Slavery. Then at last, in the autumn
of 1822, he made up his mind, and, when Wilberforce and Macaulay came to Cromer Hall to
make a final effort at persuasion, he forestalled
them with his decision to accept the leadership.
It was an historic meeting, like that other meeting of three friends under the Holmwood oak :
and Buxton's decision had all the more force of
will behind it because it had not been lightly
made. Henceforth, while other zealots laboured
behind the scenes to furnish him with arms and
armour as they had furnished Wilberforce, the
dust and heat of the public fight for Abolition
were mainly borne by him.

Their leader chosen, the Abolitionists at once
began the work of planning their campaign.
The forces at their disposal were far stronger
than those that had been mustered to begin the
fight against the Slave Trade. The Committee
of 1785 had numbered only twelve, of whom

nine were Quakers, and none was experienced in public agitation or eminent in politics. In the Anti-Slavery Society of 1823 there was again a kernel of Quakers, but around it was gathered a large and distinguished company of public men. The Duke of Gloucester was president, and among the vice-presidents were five members of the House of Lords and fourteen of the Commons, including not only the " Old Guard "—Wilberforce, Clarkson, W. Smith, Babington and Stephen—but such valuable recruits as Buxton and Brougham. This contrast between 1785 and 1823 is significant. The abolition of the Slave Trade had not of itself brought about the abolition of Slavery, but it had smoothed the way to its achievement. The first campaign had awakened the British conscience ; it had rallied recruits of all sorts and stations to the humanitarian movement ; it had educated the public mind so that it was ready to respond to a second call in the same cause ; and, incidentally, it had taught the Abolitionists the technique of agitation. Smoothly and quickly, therefore, propaganda on the old lines was set on foot. Clarkson and other stalwarts toured the country. Branches of the Society were established in provincial centres. Petitions were set flowing towards Westminster, 225 of them in 1823, nearly 600 in 1824. And all the time a steady output of literature was maintained, of which the most important items were the " manifesto " with which Wilberforce opened the campaign—a sub-

121

stantial pamphlet entitled *An Appeal to the Religion, Justice and Humanity of the Inhabitants of the British Empire in behalf of the Negro Slaves in the West Indies* and published in May, 1823 —and the elder Stephen's comprehensive two-volume treatise, *The Slavery of the British West India Colonies Delineated*, published in 1824. Even more effective, probably, was the new instrument of propaganda which the Abolitionists were now strong enough in personnel and funds to forge—the *Anti-Slavery Monthly Reporter*, which first appeared in 1823 and was edited after 1825 by Macaulay. It provided a regular up-to-date arsenal of facts, and of facts which, unlike those in some other propagandist organs, could be relied on because they had been collected or reviewed by an editor who was as scrupulous as he was indefatigable. " Whatever Macaulay says," it was freely admitted, " may be taken for gospel and quoted." Thus from 1823 onwards, public opinion throughout Britain was subjected year by year to the same sort of continuous pressure as had been brought to bear on it from 1785 to 1792, and with the same object of convincing Parliament of the need for drastic legislative action.

The strength of the opposition, on the other hand, was no greater in 1823, if anything it was weaker, than at the time of its defeat in 1807. There was more sound and fury, it is true, in the planters' resistance to this second and more drastic interference with their life and liveli-

hood ; and their champions in London, the West
India Committee, still commanded the votes
of a powerful sectional group in the House of
Commons and still had behind them the " vested
interests " of all those who owned property in
the islands or held mortgages thereon. But the
value and therefore the weight of those interests
had been undermined by insuperable economic
forces. The inevitable decline of the British
" sugar islands " had already begun by 1807 and
was now proceeding apace. Exhaustion of the
soil and the competition of foreign sugar from
Cuba and Brazil and of beet-sugar in Europe
were depressing their one staple industry to
depths from which no artificial aids, no bounties
on export, no lowering of import duties, could
now do much to raise it. Lost causes are apt to
be unpopular ; and, though the cause of Slavery
was not yet quite lost, the steady impoverish-
ment of its upholders in the islands was bound
to cool the sympathies of anyone who doubted
the expediency, in politics as in finance, of
" throwing good money after bad." The " West
Indians " now, moreover, had enemies in the
sugar-trade itself. East Indian sugar, though
inferior in quality, was capable of improvement,
and it was so much more cheaply produced that
only the imposition of a special duty to protect
its older rival prevented it from capturing a large
part of the British market. Now, Englishmen
in British India were debarred from owning
slaves, and the Company, though not yet pre-

pared to attack the delicate question of Indian
slavery, had shown its philanthropic principles
by freeing all slave-born children from 1818 onwards in St. Helena, Ceylon and Bencoolen, then
under its control. More or less sincerely, therefore, the " East Indians " in their attack on the
" West Indians "—for their demand for equal
fiscal treatment was nothing less—could join
forces with the Abolitionists and raise the cry
of " free-grown " versus " slave-grown " sugar ;
and their parliamentary leader, Thomas Whit-
more, who was certainly sincere, became one of
the vice-presidents of the Anti-Slavery Society.
Thus in the battle over Slavery, as in the last
stage of the battle over the Trade, commercial
interests were not all on one side.

It opened in the House of Commons on March
19, 1823, and again the first move was a petition
from the Quakers, presented by Wilberforce.
Then on May 15 Buxton took the field with a
long, bold, well-argued speech at the close of
which he moved

that the state of Slavery is repugnant to the principles of the British constitution and of the Christian
religion and that it ought to be gradually abolished
throughout the British colonies with as much expedition as may be found consistent with a due regard
to the well-being of the parties concerned.

In the ensuing debate the contrast with earlier
days was manifest again. Nobody dared to say
that Slavery was a necessity or that it could not

be abolished. All that Charles Ellis, the " West Indian " leader, could ask was that the process of abolition should be just such a process as the Abolitionists themselves had hitherto, but now no longer, expected and desired, a " progressive amelioration " which would " slide insensibly into general freedom," and " emancipation of which not the slaves but the masters would be willing instruments." But the most significant change was in the attitude of the Government. Canning, its spokesman as Foreign Secretary and leader of the House, was not obliged, as Pitt had been obliged, to leave the question open. Denouncing the evils of Slavery almost as vigorously as Buxton, he declared that the Government desired and intended its abolition. " Effectual and decisive measures " of amelioration would be framed, and by the " determined and persevering but at the same time judicious and temperate enforcement " of them abolition would be gradually achieved. The words sounded well, but Buxton would have preferred something more drastic and promising more rapid results. He withdrew his motion, however, for the House was obviously with Canning ; and indeed he could hardly have expected the Government or Parliament to take more vigorous action at the very outset of the campaign. The abolition of Slavery, after all, was a revolution in the social and economic life of the West Indies. Was it fair for Parliament to use its imperial power to impose it without giving the colonists one more chance of bringing it about themselves ? Was it wise for Parliament to take such action until the great majority of its members were convinced of its necessity beyond a doubt ? The process of conviction was to take ten years ; but it was complete conviction ; and the similar process required for the abolition of the Slave Trade had taken more than twice ten years.

The application of Canning's policy passed through three distinct phases, the first of which began when Lord Bathurst, the Colonial Secretary, sent copies of the resolutions and of Canning's speech to all the West Indian Governors together with a copy of a dispatch addressed to the Governor of Demerara in which he expressed the hope that the reforms indicated would be willingly and quickly adopted, especially the prohibition of the whip for " driving " gangs at work or punishing female slaves. The reaction to this dispatch was immediate and instructive. Exasperated in particular by the suggestion to discard the whip, which they regarded, as Macaulay said, as " the grand badge of Slavery," the planters exceeded their previous efforts in denouncing all interference from England. One member of the Jamaica Assembly moved a request for the dismissal of Bathurst : others demanded the secession of Jamaica from the Empire ; and an address was finally carried declaring that the existing slave-code did all that was practically possible to make the slaves " as happy and comfortable in every respect as the labouring class in any part of the world." A few weeks later, the Jamaican authorities were convinced that these happy and comfortable slaves were plotting an insurrection; and on absurdly inadequate evidence eleven of them were hanged. In Barbados, also, passion ran high, but it vented itself not on the slaves but on William Shrewsbury, a Methodist missionary, who was accused of defaming the planters in his reports to England. A body of rioters, mostly "poor whites," set themselves to interrupt his services and disperse his congregation, and, finding that the magistrates gave him no protection, they demolished his chapel and forced him to leave the island.

This violence and cruelty were not only due to anger at interference from England but also, and perhaps mainly, to fear of its effect on the slaves. And such fear, if exaggerated, was not without all grounds. The Abolitionists themselves would not have recommended the summary abolition of the whip, at any rate without making sure that the slaves understood exactly what was and was not being done. As it was, delay in publishing Bathurst's dispatch gave rise once more to excited and exaggerated notions. Again the old rumour, derived from planters' talk, ran round—that the masters were withholding the King's gift of freedom. And in one colony the results were serious. In Demerara some 13,000 slaves rebelled, seized and locked up the white men on their estates, searched their houses for arms, and killed two overseers who resisted them. There was no other looting and no arson. The troops were called out, and in the course of a few days' fighting one soldier was wounded and a hundred slaves killed. The rebels, on the whole, showed remarkable restraint, largely owing to the influence of a trusted missionary, John Smith, of the London Missionary Society; but their punishment was heavy. Martial law was continued for several months, and in the course of it 47 slaves were hanged and many others flogged and imprisoned. Five months after the rising, when hot blood might have cooled, three slaves were sentenced to 1,000 lashes apiece, two of them thereafter to work in chains for life, the third for seven years. Smith was tried for inciting the rebellion and condemned to death with a recommendation to mercy which the Governor referred to England. Before an answer was received, Smith, who was consumptive and suffering from his long confinement, died in gaol.

When the news of these disturbances reached England, the first effect was damaging to the Abolitionist cause. All the old abuse of its leaders was heard again. They were even accused of instigating the Demerara rising. " I much question," wrote Buxton, " whether there is a more unpopular individual than myself in the House." Not unnaturally, in such an atmosphere, the Government, while it was not to be bullied into abandoning its declared policy altogether, decided that its further application should be slow and cautious ; and the second phase of it, announced by Canning on March 16, 1824, was the enactment of an Order-in-Council which laid down a new and detailed code of regulations for the treatment of slaves. A great advance on any existing code, it provided for an official " protector and guardian of slaves " to act for them in all major legal proceedings, it admitted under safeguards the evidence of slaves in court, it prohibited the use of the whip for " driving " at work or for the punishment of females, it limited the amount of corporal punishment and required a record of it to be kept, it forbade the break-up of families by sale and it facilitated marriage and manumission. It was, in fact, a whole-hearted programme of " amelioration." But it was only to be introduced in the Crown Colonies, in Trinidad at once and afterwards in the other three. Towards the other colonies and their legislatures Canning proposed to continue his policy of " temperate but authoritative admonition," trusting, yet once again, that they would voluntarily adopt the reforms imposed on Trinidad. The response was as quick and tren- chant as before. The Jamaica Assembly, though the wealthier planters were now in favour of reform, decisively and repeatedly rejected a Bill for admitting slave-evidence and declared that the time was " unfavourable for the adoption of any measures interfering with long-established institutions." The Barbados Assembly passed, indeed, a new slave-law, but it was so inadequate, on some points actually worsening the slave's position, that it was promptly vetoed in London. In sum it may be said that by 1826 virtually nothing had been done by way of " amelioration " except in three or four of the lesser islands with small slave-populations such as Tobago, St. Vincent and St. Christopher.

It might have seemed, therefore, that the outbreak which had greeted the first phase of the policy of 1823 had resulted in reducing it in its second phase to a nullity. But in fact the check to the anti-Slavery movement was only temporary. For moderate-minded men were now beginning to wonder whether in fact " amelioration " could ever succeed, whether each step was not bound to provoke in the future, as it had invariably done in the past, controversy and bitterness among the planters and restlessness and risings among the slaves, and whether indeed this latter danger was not steadily increasing and becoming an argument not, as the planters said, for delaying emancipation but for hastening it. Such thoughts were driven home when in the course of three successive sessions the House of Commons was compelled to listen to a detailed and devastating recital of what the planters could do and had done under the existing system. In 1824 the Smith case was reviewed, and, when Brougham had made the most of a theme on which both his legal acumen and his powers of invective were at their best, none of his audience could pretend that Smith's trial had been anything but a tragic parody of justice. In 1825 the persecution of Shrewsbury was described, mainly again by Brougham, and the point was stressed that he had been unable to obtain the ordinary protection of the law. In 1826 Denman raised the question of the executions in Jamaica and had no difficulty in showing that the slaves had been hanged on evidence that would not have allowed of their detention in an English police-court. In all three cases there could be no real defence. By cool and clever speeches Canning succeeded in preventing the passage of sweeping motions of censure on the colonial administrations; but the Abolitionists, none the less, had won the battle, or rather the planters had won it for them. The things they had done were a plain violation of one of the most deeply-rooted English traditions, the respect for law and justice; and it seemed an intolerable anomaly that British subjects anywhere in the Empire should be exposed to such illegal and unjust treatment. On the Jamaica case a West Indian member confessed " there was only one feeling in the House, that such a state of law was utterly indefensible." But it was Smith's fate that made the strongest impression, outside the House as well as in it. It has been likened in its effect on public sentiment to the fate of John Brown, and it may well have been the decisive factor in starting the last irresistible current of anti-Slavery opinion.

The new impetus showed itself in a petition

for Abolition signed by 72,000 of the people of
London and presented in the spring of 1826.
" This House must do the work themselves,"
said Buxton in support of it, " or suffer it to be
altogether abandoned." But Canning was determined to make a third and last effort to justify
the now widely discredited policy of 1823. The
Trinidad Order-in-Council was embodied in a
Bill which the Crown officials in all the colonies
were instructed to introduce in their legislative
assemblies ; and to give greater force to this
move the House of Lords was invited to confirm
the resolutions of 1823. The Lords were willing
enough. Even so high a Tory as Lord Chancellor Eldon, who had defended the Slave Trade
to the last, could not now defend Slavery.
" For God's sake," he said, " let the system be
abolished as soon as it can be safely and practically effected." But even now, even with all
the new evidence of British public opinion con-
fronting them, the planters would not yield.
They instantly repudiated the official Bills, and
insisted on continuing to amend and consolidate
their own slave-codes for themselves ; but in
almost every instance the product of their
labours omitted this or that factor in " amelioration " which was regarded as essential by the
British Government and Parliament. For a
year or two the farce continued. " The progress of the colonies is so slow," said Brougham
in the Commons in 1828, " as to be imperceptible
to all human eyes save their own." But the

planters had done something. They had made it impossible for anyone, however patient, however moderate-minded, to retain a vestige of belief in the policy of 1823.

That Parliament did not react more quickly to the openly contumacious attitude of the colonies in 1826 was mainly due to the unstable condition of domestic politics. There was a rapid succession of Governments. Canning became Prime Minister in April, 1827, and died in August. He was succeeded by Goderich, and Goderich by Wellington. And all these Governments were mainly preoccupied with internal issues—first Catholic Emancipation and then Reform. These later Tory ministries, moreover, were less liberal-minded than Canning's, and some members of them—Peel was one—seemed less inclined than Canning to recognize that " amelioration " was meant to lead to " abolition." Sir George Murray, indeed, Wellington's Colonial Secretary, was content, as he put it, " to abstain from any extraordinary activity " at promoting even " amelioration." But none of this meant that the Abolitionist cause was at a standstill in those years. Murray himself confessed in a confidential dispatch to the colonial Governors that, unless their legislatures gave some slight practical proof of agreement with the principles of 1823, " it will soon become difficult and inadvisable, if not impossible, to stem the impatience of the people of these kingdoms." Nor was material lacking to sustain

133

and aggravate that impatience. Once more, just when it needed it, the cause got help from its enemies. Yet another exhibition of the evils of the slave-system was presented to the British public, not by West Indian planters this time, but by the French planters of Mauritius. Not only had they maintained a steady smuggling-trade in slaves from Madagascar and East Africa, but their treatment of their slaves was peculiarly brutal; and, though Mauritius was a Crown Colony, its Governor in his anxiety to placate the bitter anti-British attitude of the planters had failed to carry out the Secretary of State's instructions to apply the Trinidad model of "amelioration." The "Mauritius Case," in fact, was a scandal, and, while Macaulay aired it exhaustively and authoritatively in the columns of the *Reporter*, Buxton displayed it in all its ugly detail in the House of Commons. So hard indeed did Buxton work at this subject that his health broke down and for more than a year he was out of action. But he resumed the attack in 1828, and the Government, having made its own inquiries, was soon forced to admit that the charges he made were true. So, once more, Parliament and public opinion received a healthy shock. All the other propaganda against Slavery, declared George Stephen, had only produced a fraction "of the excitement and indignation provoked by the result of this inquiry."

Thus in 1830 the movement for freeing the British system of representative government from its old abuses and the movement for abolishing the old British slave-system came to a head together. On May 15 a great meeting of the Anti-Slavery Society was held in London. On Clarkson's motion, Wilberforce, now over 70 and very frail, took the chair. Brougham and other leaders were on the platform and Buxton moved the usual resolution for Abolition " at the earliest period." But it was soon clear that for the younger and larger part of the audience this was not enough. In spite of protests from the " elder statesmen " deprecating hasty and violent courses, an amendment demanding immediate Abolition was carried in a tempest of cheering. It was asking, of course, for the impossible. The crisis of Reform was at hand, and in those preoccupied and dangerous days in England it was absurd to ask Lord Grey and his colleagues to deal with Slavery overseas. Even in 1831, however, they did something : they gave one more jerk to the machinery of " amelioration," now practically at a standstill. A revised and stiffened Order-in-Council was imposed on all the Crown Colonies, and the " legislative " Colonies were told that, if they would adopt this Order as their slave-code, the lowering of duties on their sugar-trade, which they had so long and urgently desired, would be conceded them. It is scarcely necessary to state the sequel. Not even the victory of the Whigs could teach the planters that the sands were running out. In the Crown Colonies the new Order was met with organized opposition. Lawyers and merchants joined the planters in demanding its suspension. In St. Lucia the store-keepers closed their shops for a week. In the other colonies the new bribe was quite as fiercely repudiated as the old admonitions and rebukes. In Jamaica it was proposed to raise a permanent militia as a step to securing annexation to the United States. Everywhere else the British Government's proposal was as promptly and bluntly rejected. Only little St. Christopher condescended to make an excuse—its poverty. And precisely as before and for precisely the same reasons this violent agitation of the whites was followed by restlessness among the blacks. The trouble came to a head in Jamaica at the end of the year. In January 1832, some 50,000 slaves broke loose. Three or four whites were murdered or burned in their houses. Ten were killed in the fighting. Of the rebels about 400 were killed and about 100 executed. The missionaries, though again no charge of incitement could be substantiated, were again denounced as the authors of the rising. Several of them were mobbed and expelled. Fourteen chapels were destroyed. The old story, in fact, was repeated, word for word, to its bitter end. But its moral was now quite changed. Most Englishmen had come to regard these tragic outbreaks not as discrediting but as justifying the case for Abolition.

Meantime that case was being argued more

fully and widely than ever before. Except in the winter of 1831–2, the most dangerous phase of the Reform struggle, the Anti-Slavery Society in London and its branches in all the larger towns continued their intensive propaganda. In 1831 the agitation was given a keener edge by a so-called Agency Committee which represented the younger and more radical Abolitionists. Mainly run by George Stephen and three Quakers, Emanuel and Joseph Cooper and Joseph Sturge, and mainly financed by Quaker money, it employed " agents," paid and unpaid, whom it briefed with the Abolition case and sent to lecture all over the country. Women as well as men were sent campaigning—a startling novelty which occasioned some shaking of older heads. One petition, bearing 187,000 signatures, was largely the work of two women canvassers. The effects were substantial, especially in the Midlands, where Sturge's influence radiated from his home in Birmingham. Within a year the number of affiliated Societies rose from 200 to 1,300. Nor was the advocacy of Abolition restricted now to the professional Abolitionists. Sermons were preached against Slavery in many churches. Leading newspapers, hitherto hostile or neutral, began to give active support. Among the solid reviews, much more influential in politics then than now, the *Quarterly*, mouthpiece of unbending Toryism, had given up the planters in despair, and the *Edinburgh* and the *Westminster* were warmly anti-Slavery. But it must not be supposed that the forces of Abolition had the field to themselves. Well aware that the final battle was now joined, the " West Indians " fought as stubbornly as ever. They, too, had their Standing Committee and their *Reporter*, and they, too, had money at their back. They pursued the Abolition " agents " with counter-propaganda, denying the truth of their attacks on Slavery, questioning their figures, asserting the rights of property, appealing to conservative instincts to save the lives and fortunes of loyal colonists from the new Jacobins and the Black Terror they invoked. One arresting device was their invention : they placarded London walls with pro-Slavery bills at night ; whereupon George Stephen organized a " flying-squad " of bill-stickers who pasted anti-Slavery bills on top of them before the morning.

In Parliament, meantime, the cause had been gaining votes. Several "West Indians," identifying the claims of property in slaves and in " rotten boroughs," had lost their seats at the general election on Reform, while several successful candidates had pledged themselves to Abolition. The Irish members, led by O'Connell, were all the more ready to back the " Saints " because some of the " Saints " had backed Catholic Emancipation. And the " East Indians " were still at odds with the " West Indians " on the sugar duties. But the rank and file of the Whig majority in the Commons were loyal to the Government, and the Government, overwhelmed with other problems crying out for treatment, still postponed the fate of Slavery. When Buxton courageously insisted on dividing the House in the spring of 1832 on the question of immediate Abolition, he was beaten by 136 to 92 ; and, though this minority was so substantial that the Government—so at least said Lord Althorp, one of its strongest members— would have to yield to it, nothing was done before the new elections in December, and after them no mention was made of Slavery in the King's Speech. And Buxton became still more uneasy when Goderich was transferred from the Colonial Office and Howick, his under-secretary, resigned, both being staunch Abolitionists ; and when Stanley, the new Colonial Secretary, markedly asserted his independence of Henry Taylor, the worst enemy of Slavery among the officials in the department, and of James Stephen the Second, its legal adviser, who had inherited his father's notorious opinions. It was soon evident, however, that public opinion would brook no more delay. A young Yorkshire business-man, named Whitely, had just returned, as it happened, from a few weeks' sojourn on a Jamaica plantation. He related what he had seen, especially the floggings of the slaves, to Buxton, who persuaded him to put his story into print. There was nothing new in the little pamphlet, but its effect on public feeling, already heated by Abolitionist propaganda, was a conflagration. In a fortnight nearly 200,000 copies were sold.

Further efforts by George Stephen's Agency Committee — lectures, newspaper - articles, public meetings, sermons—added fuel to the flames. Petitions poured in to Parliament with nearly 1,500,000 signatures. And when anti-Slavery delegates from every local centre in the country were summoned to a great convention at Exeter Hall on April 18, 1833, Buxton needed all his tact and force of character to restrain them from demanding instant Abolition without compromise or safeguard, leaving the planters without any set-off to their loss of property and the plantations without labourers to till them. When the delegates proceeded in a body to Downing Street to present an address to the Prime Ministers, neither Althorp nor Stanley, who received them, nor any of their colleagues could evade the fact that these 330 men, coming from all parts of the country and from every rank and calling, were voicing the determined and now at last impatient demand of the great majority of the British people.

Ministers, of course, had always sympathized with the Abolitionists in principle, and the Government scheme, propounded by Stanley on May 14, was a sufficiently drastic measure. All the indirect methods of bringing Slavery to an end by "amelioration," serfdom, or manumission were discarded. The angry protests of the "West Indians," their appeals for more delay, their threats of secession were swept aside. It was proposed that the legal status of Slavery should cease within a year; but that, to ease the shock to their owners, all existing slaves over six years old should continue to serve as unpaid "apprentices" for three-quarters of the working day for twelve years, while the planters would be compensated for the loss of a quarter of their unpaid labour by a loan of £15 million from the British Treasury. For the remainder of the day the "apprentice" could, if he chose, work for wages and thus earn the means of purchasing his release at a valuation. The resolutions embodying this scheme were carried by comfortable majorities; and Stanley, as if to prove that the long years of procrastination were really over, pressed on its passage into law. Stephen, whose collaboration could no longer be dispensed with, drafted the Bill in two days and a half—one of the two sole occasions in his life on which, true child of the "Clapham Sect," he consented to work on Sunday—and on July 5 it was introduced. During its course through Parliament, only two substantial changes were made. In deference to Buxton and his party, who opposed the plan of apprenticeship altogether, its period was reduced to six years for "predial" or field-labour and to four years for "non-predial" labour. In compliance with the "West Indian" demand, the £15 million was increased to £20 million and made a free gift instead of a loan. Except for the "West Indians" and stubborn Tories like Wellington, it was only on these minor issues and not on that of Abolition itself that there was now any open division of opinion in either House. On August 29 the Abolition of Slavery Bill became law.

By a dramatic coincidence the great veteran of the cause lay dying while the Bill was being debated. " When Mr. Wilberforce hears of it," said Stanley, of one of the vital decisions, " he may well exclaim, ' Lord, now lettest Thou Thy servant depart in peace.' " " Thank God," said Wilberforce himself, a few days before his death on July 29, " that I should have lived to witness a day in which England is willing to give twenty millions sterling for the abolition of Slavery." At this moment also a breakdown of health put an end to the active life of another veteran, Zachary Macaulay, to whose untiring and unceasing help behind the scenes the parliamentary leaders of the cause confessed that their triumph was largely due, " the unseen ally of Mr. Wilberforce and the pillar of his strength," as Gladstone described him in after years, " my tutor all the way through," as Buxton called him on the morrow of victory.

What were the results of this great measure ? The opponents of Abolition had declared that the slaves were quite unfit for freedom and that their enfranchisement would lead to disorder, drunkenness, insubordination, and a general refusal to do any more work. None of this came true. When at midnight on July 31, 1834, the historic moment came, there were celebrations and rejoicings, but the ex-slaves behaved with decency and order : and, though the new apprenticeship seemed something much less than real freedom, they accepted it nearly everywhere obediently and in some colonies cheerfully. There was nothing like a general " strike." The output of sugar between 1834 and 1838 fell from the average level of the previous six years by less than ten per cent. The difficulty, indeed, in operating the rather complicated system of apprenticeship was not so much due to the Negroes as to the planters. They had not been ungenerously treated in the settlement of 1833. Years of open defiance had not impaired the British sense of justice, and Parliament had done what it could to soften the blow of emancipation by conceding the apprenticeship-system and pecuniary compensation. If the money given was only about half the market-value of the slaves, it was more than their owners had hoped for ; and, if Parliament had accepted the argument of the extremists that no rights could be attached to property in human beings, the planters might have found themselves, like the slave-owners in England after the Somerset judgement, with no compensation at all. Some of them were ready to face the facts and try to make the best of the new system, but others—and again the worst offenders were in Jamaica—not only abused such masters' powers as were left them but evaded and even infringed the regulations which had been laid down as the condition of their receiving compensation. Once more they wrought their own undoing. Again there was constant friction between the Jamaican Assembly and the Governors; again conditions in all the islands were forced on public attention in England. In 1836 Sturge himself, the chief opponent of apprenticeship, paid a visit to the islands, and, though his descriptions of what he saw there were often exaggerated and unfair, they were none the less effective propaganda. It was widely, though untruly, said that the Negroes were worse off as apprentices then they had been as slaves; and much was made of the fact that the planters of Antigua had voluntarily emancipated their 30,000 slaves in 1834 and had since maintained their full output of sugar with wholly free labour. Moderate opinion, accordingly, began to swing into line. Early in 1838 both Brougham and Buxton declared for the cessation of apprenticeship; and a second Abolition Act would soon have been making its way through Parliament if the planters had not forestalled it. They had no great liking themselves for the apprenticeship system; they foresaw the difficulties and unsettlement that would be created when the "non-predial" slaves, a sixth of the total, became quite free in the summer of 1838, leaving their comrades in apprenticeship; and they resented the idea of being a second time overridden by imperial legislation. So, one after another, Jamaica last but one, they were persuaded to follow Antigua's lead; and August 1, 1838, was another great day for the Negroes. Their rejoicing this time was more whole-hearted, but they were as orderly and sober as before, and again their churches and chapels were crowded. " I never beheld," wrote the Bishop of Jamaica, " a more impressive and affecting scene."

For the planters, of course, emancipation told a different story. To the growing pressure of foreign competition was now added the failure of their labour supply. The ex-slaves were not all unwilling to work on the estates, but they preferred to work for themselves, if they could, and not for their ex-masters. And on this point the experience of Antigua had been misleading, since almost all the cultivable land in that colony was already occupied and more or less developed, so that the freedmen could find little means of subsistence except in their previous employment. It was the same in Barbados, but in most of the other colonies, including Jamaica, there were large waste areas of virgin soil, and, naturally enough, the freed apprentices preferred to lease or, better still, to buy small plots of their own on which the idle could grow enough foodstuffs to live on and the energetic enough to get at least as much profit from their marketing as they would get by earning wages at toilsome sugar-cultivation. Exemplary planters might still attract sufficient labour, but most Negroes were now unwilling to be hired for more than three or four days a week or more than seven hours a day. The result was a steep decline in produc-

tion. Sympathetic British Governments tried to
check it by assisting in the organized immigration of labour from oversea—slaves caught by
cruisers and freed, paupers from Madeira, and
even, with tragic results, peasants from England
—but all these efforts failed. The importation
of "indentured" coolies under official supervision from India was more effective, especially
in Trinidad and Guiana; but it was too costly
and uncertain to stop the rot. And in 1846 came
the final blow. Extended in 1825 to Mauritian
and at last in 1836 to "East Indian" sugar, the
British preference on West Indian sugar was
swept away by the great tide of Free Trade; and
—an ironical comment on earlier anti-Slavery
doctrine—the sugar of the British islands, though
now it was triumphantly "free-grown," was
forced to fight for its life in equal competition
with "slave-grown" sugar from Cuba and Brazil.
Many of the older generation of planters suc-
cumbed, and it was only by the advent of new
men, new methods, and new crops, especially
fruit, that the islands eventually held their own.
But the glory had departed, never to return. In
the eighteenth century the British West Indies
had been the pearls of the imperial crown; but
their brilliance had been artificially sustained by
the slave-system and the Mercantile System, and,
when both those systems disappeared, the sun
went down and the islands faded out of history.
Sunset for 70,000 white men, but dawn for
700,000 black. No need for sentimentalists to

+ "why make such a fuss
about admitting slave-grown sugar when you are wearing
slave-grown cotton, drinking slave-grown coffee, smoking
or snuffing slave-grown tobacco"

gild the picture : it is certain that, though the pace presently slowed down, the progress of the Negroes continued after 1838. Some of them, of course, reverted more or less to barbarism. There were plenty of idlers and vagabonds. But, speaking broadly, the freedmen converted themselves with remarkable rapidity into a stable, contented and not unprosperous peasant-community. They congregated in " free villages " and increasingly acquired the ownership of their land. Family life became more common, and the old fall of population gave place to a steady rise. The improvement in the standard of living, in clothing, housing, furniture and the like, was reflected for a time in the doubling of the imports of manufactured goods from England. In many parts they paid for their children's education, and in some they were well enough off to contribute large sums for building churches. " I venture to say," wrote Governor Metcalfe in 1841, " that in no country in the world can the labouring population be more abundantly provided with the necessaries and comforts of life, more at their ease, or more secure from oppression, than in Jamaica." Planters themselves admitted the improvement. Most of those who gave evidence before a parliamentary committee in 1842 spoke highly of all the Negroes' qualities except their unwillingness to work for wages. In Jamaica, said one of them, they had made " a more rapid advance in the scale of humanity than probably

any set of persons ever did in a similar period."
Nor, finally, had the contrasted fortunes of black
and white engendered bitterness between the
races. On the contrary, despite all that had
passed, relations between the planters on the one
side and the Negroes and even the detested
missionaries on the other were better than they
had ever been. And if in some degree this dawn
of a new age was a false dawn, if the Negroes
failed to maintain the heights they reached in the
first inspiring years of freedom, nevertheless the
general conditions of their life and their prospects
of future progress remained immeasurably better
than in the deadening days of Slavery.

In Mauritius the results of emancipation were
different. The planters fared better ; the ex-
slaves worse. The planters were able to evade
the worst effects of emancipation because, being
so near India, they were able to obtain a regular
and adequate supply of " coolies." In Mauritius
alone of all the sugar-colonies the output of sugar
immediately after 1838 actually rose, and even
after 1846 Mauritius did better on the whole than
the West Indies. Of the 60,000 or 70,000 ex-
slaves, on the other hand, while the " non-pre-
dials " mostly continued to work as artisans for
wages or on their own account, the great agricultural majority failed to create for themselves
any organized society or even to earn a decent
livelihood. They drifted into vagrancy, thiev-
ing, and destitution, and presently lost contact
with the civilized life of the island. When a

rather conscience-stricken Colonial Office inquired about them in 1845, it seemed as if the only certain thing known about them was that their number had greatly decreased.

The only other British colony affected by slave-emancipation was Cape Colony, and here again its results were different. The loss of some 39,000 slaves was a serious blow to their owners, and it was aggravated by the reduction of the compensation as assessed from over £2½ million to less than £1¼ million and by the unsatisfactory methods of its payment. Some owners were ruined, many were hard hit. But the circumstances at the Cape were quite unlike those in the West Indies. It was part of Africa, and the slaves were a tiny body in the mass of Africans—Hottentots established in the Colony, Bantu pressing down from the north—into which, when freed, they merged themselves. Nor did their masters rely, like Jamaican planters, on a single crop nor on any crop requiring such intensive cultivation as sugar. The results of emancipation, indeed, were less economic in Cape Colony than political. The Act of 1833 was regarded by the more recalcitrant Dutch farmers, the free-spirited, old-fashioned pioneers of the frontier, as the worst of a series of measures imposed on them by a far-off ignorant Government at the bidding of pious fanatics. It was not that they were wedded to Slavery as an institution ; but they regarded its abolition as inspired, like the previous measures, by the in-

old Dutch Calvinism coming out.

tolerable doctrine that heathen blacks and Christian whites should be treated on a footing of equality. Emancipation, therefore, was one of the grievances, as some of their leaders confessed, which precipitated the Great Trek of 1835–6, when several thousand Boers " trekked " away beyond the colonial border to found free republics of their own in inner Africa on the basic principle that " there shall be no equality between black and white in Church or State."

nB. work of the African Institution 1807-26.

nB. Effect of humanitarian movement on Hottentots and Kaffirs etc in S. Africa.

CHAPTER VI

THE FIGHT WITH THE FOREIGN SLAVE TRADE

THE final abolition of the British Slave Trade in 1811 and the final abolition of British Slavery in 1838 destroyed a substantial part of the old slave-system but by no means all of it. In 1838 Slavery still existed not only in native Africa and in many parts of Asia but also in areas occupied or controlled by the Christian West— in the French, Spanish and Portuguese colonies, in the southern section of the United States, and in the young republics of South America. The remaining chapters of this book will be concerned with the efforts made by the British people, having abandoned their own great share in the slave-system, to secure its abandonment by other peoples.

The first of these efforts was directed against the Trade which fed the slave-plantations of foreign countries and colonies on the other side of the Atlantic. Some States had already like Britain forsworn the Trade before the end of the war. In 1804 an Act, which had been passed in 1792 to abolish the Danish Trade in twelve years' time, came into force. Sweden enacted Abolition in 1813 and Holland in 1814. Similar

151

action, meantime, had been taken in America. In the United States the opposition of South Carolina and Georgia, the two chief slave-States, had prevented the Convention of 1787 from immediately abolishing the Slave Trade in the terms of the Federal Constitution, and as a compromise—foreshadowing already the great schism of 1861—it was enacted that " the migration or importation of such persons as any of the States now existing think proper to admit shall not be prohibited by Congress prior to the year 1808." In the interval all the northern and central States separately outlawed the Trade, and several of them did away with Slavery also. Even Georgia and, for a period, South Carolina prohibited slave-importation, mainly for fear lest disaffected slaves from the West Indies and raw slaves from Africa might incite a repetition of the recent slave-revolt in Haiti. Illicit traffic, however, especially to stock the plantations of newly acquired Louisiana, continued, and when in 1803 South Carolina reopened her ports nearly 40,000 slaves were landed at Charleston in the course of four years. Meanwhile the Abolition movement had gathered strength in the North, with the Quakers as usual to the fore, and on March 2, 1807, twenty-three days before George III assented to the British Bill, President Jefferson approved a measure of Congress, prohibiting as from January 1, 1808, the importation of slaves into the United States from abroad and penalizing all participation in such trade, but, in order to enable slaves to be sold between State and State, allowing the coastwise trade to continue in ships over forty tons. Further Acts were passed, in 1818 stiffening the penalties and adding imprisonment, in 1819 providing for the payment of "prize-money," and in 1820 declaring the Trade piracy and a capital offence. In South America Venezuela, Chile and Buenos Aires abolished the Trade between 1810 and 1812.

But all these measures could do little to lessen the volume, actual or potential, of the trans-Atlantic Trade as long as the chief participants, France, Spain and Portugal, continued it. During the war, indeed, it had been kept in bounds by British sea-power. French slave-ships and those of Spain and Holland as long as Napoleon kept them at war with Britain were exposed to capture by British cruisers, and that such enemy-trade continued at all was mainly due to its sailing under the "false colours" of a neutral State. But, when at last the end of the war came in sight, it was clear that, unless something were done to prevent it, the West European Trade, especially that of France, whose share of the whole business before the war had been second only to the British, would recover all its old proportions. The Abolitionist leaders did what they could to forestall this danger. "It would be shocking," said Wilberforce, "to restore to Europe the blessings of peace with professions of our principles of justice and humanity and at the same moment to be creating—for so it would really be doing wherever the Slave Trade is extinct—this traffic in the persons of our fellow-creatures." He pressed the point on Castlereagh at the Foreign Office. He wrote long letters, describing the evils of the Trade, to some of the foremost figures on the European stage—to Czar Alexander, to Talleyrand, to Von Humboldt, to Lafayette. And again as in 1807 public opinion was at Wilberforce's back in overwhelming force. On the eve of the peace-settlement 800 petitions with nearly a million signatures called on the House of Commons to prevent the renewal of the French Slave Trade, and the House accepted without dividing Wilberforce's motions for strong action at the Congress of Vienna. Never has a British diplomat taken with him to a great international conference so clear or so strong a mandate as Castlereagh took to Vienna. The great body of British opinion was not deeply interested in the primary task that awaited him and his fellow-statesmen—the immense task of re-shaping the map of Europe and laying the foundations of peace after more than twenty years of war. It was deeply, almost fiercely, interested in one thing only—the general abolition of the Slave Trade throughout the world. The demand indeed was expressed with such a loud and unanimous voice as to be diplomatically embarrassing. The " display of popular impatience " on this single aim, said Castlereagh, would be used by foreign plenipotentiaries to force concessions from us on other points. But he did his best to execute his mandate, and the result was all that was practically possible at the time. Alexander, the idealist, could safely preach the gospel of humanity and Metternich, the realist, as safely acquiesce, since neither Russia nor Austria were sea-powers or participants in the Trade. Prussia was in a similar position. Sweden, like Britain, had clean hands. And even for Talleyrand and the representatives of Spain and Portugal it was possible to assert the adherence of their countries to the principle at any rate of Abolition. So on February 8, 1815, the plenipotentiaries of the Eight Powers set their hands to a joint declaration which was annexed to the Final Act, signed on June 9.

They declare [it ran], in the face of Europe, that, considering the universal abolition of the Slave Trade as a measure particularly worthy of their attention, conformable to the spirit of the times and to the generous principles of their august Sovereigns, they are animated with the sincere desire of concurring in the most prompt and effectual execution of this measure by all the means at their disposal, and of acting in the employment of these means with all the zeal and perseverance which is due to so great and noble a cause.

They added that the precise moment at whch the Trade should be abolished by any of its practitioners would be a matter of international negotiation.

British public opinion was by no means satis-

fied with the evasive ending of this high-sound-
ing manifesto; and its suspicions were soon
justified. Though it had been decided at Vienna
to hold annual conferences in order to facilitate
the Powers' " united efforts," the first was not
held till 1818 at Aix, the second not till 1822 at
Verona, and both, despite the vigorous exertions
of Castlereagh and Wellington, were virtually
fruitless. Only, it was evident, by diplomatic
pressure on individual Governments could any
real progress be achieved, and for the first thirty
years of the peace and even later the British
Foreign Office was more occupied with this
question than with any other aspect of international affairs. It not only added vastly to
the weight of a Foreign Minister's work: it
encumbered his diplomacy. That unending
stream of dispatches, those appeals, protests,
admonitions, that constant nagging—it was like
the treatment meted out to the West Indian
planters in Canning's day; and in Paris, Madrid
and Lisbon it was similarly regarded as the
outcome of British fanaticism or hypocrisy and
often no less angrily resented. No doubt the
fact that other nations were profiting from a vice
which Britain had denied herself added a zest
and a bitterness to higher motives: but foreign
critics were wrong in their belief that the main
impulse was economic, that *l'île marchande* expected to profit from its rivals' following its
lead. The abolition of the foreign Slave Trade
would primarily profit the " West Indians," and

the declining political influence of that community had been revealed in 1807 and was to be still more clearly exposed in 1833 and 1846. Throughout those years of controversy, indeed, the diplomatic representatives of Britain were as well aware as Castlereagh had been at Vienna that their policy was dictated by no sordid or sectional " interest " but by a public opinion which hated the Trade for the simple reason that, thanks to the propaganda of the Abolitionists, they knew so much about its evils ; and, if they were obliged to be importunate and at times discourteous to foreign Governments, at any rate they knew that they were only asking other countries to do what in " the face of Europe " they had promised to do and what Britain alone among the great European Powers had honestly done.

The most powerful of the surviving slave-trading countries, and therefore the most difficult to deal with, was France. In 1814 the British Government had hoped that the French Slave Trade, which had been completely stopped by the war, would not be restarted, especially as its chief bases in African waters, the colonies of Senegal, Goree, Île de France and Bourbon, which had been taken by Britain from the Napoleonic Empire, were now being restored, the third excepted, to the Bourbon monarchy. But the French would only agree to suppress the Trade at the end of five years, and the old slave-ports — Nantes, Havre, Bordeaux,

Marseilles—were soon busily engaged in fitting out ships to reap what profits they could in the time allowed them. Then came a dramatic change. Napoleon, breaking from Elba and making a throw for British sympathy, decreed the immediate abolition of the Trade ; and after Waterloo Louis XVIII's ministers, pressed hard by Wellington, undertook to replace the usurper's decree with a " legitimist " ordinance and signed the second Treaty of Paris in which both France and Britain bound themselves to the execution of the declaration at Vienna and declared that they had " prohibited without restriction their colonies and subjects from taking any part whatever in this traffic." In 1817, however, the British Ambassador discovered that the publication of the prohibiting ordinance had been overlooked ; and though in the following year the Trade was made illegal by an Act of the French legislature, it was not made a crime, and consequently it proved far less effective than the British Act of 1811. Slave-ships sailed from French ports almost as openly as in the eighteenth century ; Senegal and Goree were alive with the Trade ; and " slavers," of other nations besides France, passed unmolested under the French flag. It was not till 1831, when the " Revolution of July " had put Louis Philippe on the throne, that the penalties on participation in the Trade, direct and indirect, were stiffened by new legislation and the Government set itself, for a time at least, to stamp it out.

To persuade Spain and Portugal to outlaw the Trade had been an easier task. It was mainly a matter of money, British taxpayers' money. Portugal, who enjoyed the larger share of the Trade, was induced in 1815 by the remission of £450,000 of debt owed to Britain and by the gift of £300,000, disguised as an " indemnity " for captured slave-ships, to sign a treaty which confined her Trade to the transport of slaves from Africa south of the Equator to her "possessions " across the Atlantic. This meant that, her old slave-base at Bissao being now " out of bounds," only the ports of Angola and Mozambique would be available for exporting slaves and only Brazil for their import ; and when between 1822 and 1825 Brazil became an independent state, the Portuguese Trade was brought to an end *de iure*, but not as will appear *de facto*, by the treaty-terms. Brazil for her part not only accepted the obligations inherited from Portugal but in 1831 she passed an Act providing for the punishment of slave-traders and the confiscation of their ships. To Spain, where the removal of the traditional ban on slave-trading in 1789 had opened the way to a heavy traffic especially with Cuba, similar pressure was applied with similar results. The hope that Spain would voluntarily abandon the Trade at the end of the war as a mark of gratitude for British services in the Peninsula was disappointed ; she even refused a bribe for immediate and complete abolition to the tune of £850,000 by way of gift and 10 million dollars by way of loan; but in 1817, in return for a gift of £400,000, she limited her share of the Trade to the south of the Equator—a far greater ostensible sacrifice in her case than in that of Portugal, since it cut her off from Cuba—and undertook to drop it altogether in 1820. The promise was honoured in form the Trade was duly outlawed but it was not till 1835, when Spain, like France, had obtained a more liberal form of government, that effective penalties were imposed.

Thus at the end of twenty years laws abolishing the Slave Trade, with adequate penal provisions, had been adopted by all the Powers which had continued to take part in it after 1814. But that did not mean the abolition of this foreign Trade. On the contrary, it grew enormously. All those laws, in truth, were just so much waste-paper as long as they were not enforced; and beside the countless files of dispatches penned in the Foreign Office and British Embassies abroad in order to secure the enactment of those laws lay still more voluminous files concerned with their enforcement. For the plain fact was that of all the Powers which legally " abolished " the Trade, only Britain took the requisite steps to ensure that her law was *strictly and continuously* obeyed.

As soon as the Act of 1807 came into force, though ships could ill be spared from their war-stations, a number of cruisers were dispatched to patrol the African coast, and after the war was over, this " preventive " or " African "

Squadron was maintained. Its strength was steadily increased until in the 'forties it employed about one-sixth of the British Navy and cost the British taxpayer about three-quarters of a million sterling a year. Service in it was often dangerous—for the cornered " slaver " could fight hard—and always unhealthy, especially the inshore boat-work up malarious rivers. In 1845, for instance, 5 per cent of the ships' companies were killed or died, and 10 per cent were invalided home ; and the figures were sometimes much higher. The dreary spells of inaction, moreover, when the ships lay watching that savage coast, with no change or recreation, no trips ashore, no social life, told heavily on mind and body. " The monotony of the blockade," wrote a commodore, " is killing to officers and men . . . for months at anchor, rolling terribly, thermometer 86 degrees, no change of companions, no supplies of fresh stock except at long intervals." But there were compensations. There was prize-money—£5 for every slave released and landed, £4 a ton for every empty slave-ship captured. There was the occasional excitement of a chase when the latest cruiser from a British dockyard strained sail to catch an American-built clipper whose " racehorse beauty " ill deserved the use to which it was put. And there were the deeper satisfactions of the work itself, the sense, bred of close contact with the horrors of the Trade, that a chance of coming to grips with it was worth

161

F

some risk and hardship, the sight of a captured " slaver," the joy of the rescued slaves. In officers and men alike the Trade inspired a burning hate. It was scarcely ever mentioned in dispatches without some violent epithet— this " abominable," " infamous," " diabolical " " traffic in human flesh." Captains of the old school felt themselves to be fighting God's battle with the Devil.

Armed with the Act of 1811, this British patrol very soon succeeded in driving all British ships out of the Trade. Englishmen even shrank from serving in it under foreign flags. A slave-trader of Franco-Italian parentage, after retiring from a long and prosperous business between Africa and the West Indies, declared that among all the international riff-raff composing the crews of the slave-ships he had met with, there was one " only English subject I ever knew to ship in a slaver," and he was a cabin-boy. The truth is that in a very short time the *whole* of the Trade could have been suppressed if the other maritime Powers had joined in the patrol in proportion to their naval strength, and, if that were too much to expect, it could still have been, if not wholly suppressed, at least reduced to relatively narrow limits if the other Powers had permitted Britain to do for them what they would not do themselves. Year after year the British Government pressed for the concession of a " reciprocal right of search," which meant that, as between two consenting Powers, the cruisers of either would be entitled to stop ships flying the other's flag if suspected of carrying slaves, and, if they were found to be doing so, to take them to certain ports where "Courts of Mixed Commission" would be empowered to apply the anti-Slave Trade laws of their two nations. The case for such an agreement was unanswerable, and yet it is easy to understand why it proved so difficult to obtain. Some Governments were apathetic in the matter or actually at times not unwilling that the Trade should continue even after laws against it had been passed. But the main objection lay in an intelligible jealousy of British sea-power. In theory, it was true, the British flag would be no less exposed to "insult" from a foreign cruiser than any other flag; but in practice, as long as British cruisers alone or almost alone were employed in the patrol, the "reciprocal right" would be exercised only or almost only by those arrogant British seamen whose high-handed interference with neutral shipping in the war had been notorious. There were Frenchmen, indeed, who seriously maintained that the motive of the British agitation for the right of search was not humanitarian at all but only a desire to demonstrate that Britannia ruled the waves. In such an atmosphere the task of the Foreign Office was hard and its progress slow.

To begin with Spain, the Treaty of 1817, which limited the area of her slave-trade, provided also for reciprocal search and setting-up of mixed Commission Courts at Sierra Leone and Havana. But for two reasons this was not quite the "practical abolition" which the delighted British philanthropists supposed it to be. First, the judgments of the British and Spanish members of the Courts on captured ships so often conflicted that at one time it became the custom to decide the issue by drawing lots. Second, and more important, since Spanish "slavers" could only be seized under the Treaty if they had slaves actually on board, their masters were enabled to avoid seizure either by keeping the slaves hidden on shore until nightfall or thick weather or a change of wind offered a chance of slipping through the patrol or by throwing the slaves overboard when sighted and pursued—a less desirable alternative since it meant the total loss of dozens and sometimes hundreds of valuable slaves, but often enough adopted in the last resort. In 1822, accordingly, Spain was induced to sign another treaty permitting seizure if there was evidence that slaves had been on board, but technical difficulties made it practically useless, and it was not till 1835 that the Spanish authorities, besides stiffening the penalties for those engaged in the Trade, agreed to a clause in the treaty providing for seizure if ships were found to be equipped with decks, shackles and other tackle for carrying slaves. Then, at last, the Spanish flag could no longer be relied on to protect a "slaver."

To obtain the co-operation of Portugal was

still more difficult. She had acquiesced in the right of search in 1817, but, when a replica of the Spanish Treaty of 1835 was submitted at Lisbon, signature was stubbornly refused. For three years Palmerston went on pressing his case. Portuguese ministers were willing to issue more decrees, but nothing would induce them to concede the only means by which such decrees could be given the slightest practical effect. Strong language was used. " The ships of Portugal," said Palmerston, " now prowl about the ocean, pandering to the crimes of other nations ; and when her own ships are not sufficiently numerous for the purpose, her flag is lent as a shield to protect the misdeeds of foreign pirates." Finally, despairing of Portuguese assent, the British Government brusquely—and can it be said inexcusably ?—broke all the rules of international propriety. In 1839, after due warning, it carried an Act of Parliament which provided that Portuguese vessels (and vessels not attached to any State), if found to be equipped for the Slave Trade, might be seized by British cruisers and brought in for adjudication by a British court as if they were British vessels. For three years this remarkable Act remained in force with the result that, as Palmerston had predicted, slave-trading under the Portuguese flag was practically wiped out. In 1842 Portugal at last gave in ; a treaty was signed, declaring the Trade piracy and permitting reciprocal search with an " equipment article " ; and in the next year the Act of 1839 as far as it affected Portuguese ships was repealed.

France, who had more than once contested the command of the sea with Britain, was the least likely of European Powers to acquiesce in British interference with her shipping. She flatly refused the " reciprocal right of search " when Spain and Portugal accepted it in 1817. But so marked was the change of public sentiment which inspired the Abolition law of 1831 that in the same year a search-treaty was signed with Britain and in 1833 the " equipment article " was added by a supplementary convention. Nor was the execution of these commitments left to the British Navy. French cruisers began to atone for years of inaction by a vigorous pursuit of " slavers." Unhappily, however, this phase of mutual trust and competitive energy did not last long. Partly, no doubt, owing to controversies on other issues which more than once in the 'forties strained Franco-British relations nearly to breaking-point, partly under the influence of American precept and practice, French opinion turned against the " right of search " ; and in 1845 the Treaty of 1831 was suspended and replaced by an agreement binding France and Britain each to maintain a squadron of twenty-six ships on the African coast. This determination to dispense with British help in preventing the misuse of the French flag was not unnatural, nor unjustifiable, but it required that the naval energy of the preceding period should be maintained. The French squadron, however, was soon reduced to twelve ships, and in 1848 the British commodore in West Africa reported that for the past two years no " slaver " had been held up by a French cruiser.

The attitude of the United States might seem at first sight more surprising. But it must be remembered that throughout these years the ardent humanitarian sentiment of the North was countered by the jealousies and suspicions of the South where, just as in Jamaica in earlier days, attacks on the Slave Trade were apt to be identified with attacks on Slavery, and no responsible American statesman desired at that time to widen a breach which threatened to split the Union. Would Britain, it may be asked, have been able to destroy her slave-system when she did, if it had been the mainstay of her southern counties ? It must be remembered, also, that American feelings were peculiarly sensitive on the question of British interference with other people's shipping. The arbitrary stoppage and visitation of American vessels by British warships in order to impress British subjects found thereon or to recover deserters from the British Navy had been one of the prime causes of the War of 1812, and after the peace of 1815 that particular controversy continued to be the most explosive subject in Anglo-American relations. Nor was it only a question of wounded national dignity. American opinion felt itself to be upholding the great principle of " the freedom of the seas," and to be vindicating the rights of the weaker peoples against the might of British sea-power. It is hardly, therefore, to be wondered at if the United States proved the most intransigent of all nations on the issue of the "right of search." Once only, at an early stage of the long dispute, its attitude softened: between 1822 and 1824 the concession of the "reciprocal right" was recommended by both houses of Congress but rejected by President Monroe and, when Monroe had been converted and actually signed a treaty, the Senate refused to ratify it. The chance did not recur. Foreign Secretaries in London and Ambassadors in Washington appealed in vain. They offered, if the right of search were conceded in the limited area of the Slave Trade, to renounce the right elsewhere and to forgo the claim to impress seamen on a searched ship. No use. In 1841, despairing of separate negotiations, the British Government succeeded in securing the signatures of the French, Austrian, Prussian and Russian Governments, its chief associates in the Vienna manifesto, to a reciprocal-search treaty with the idea of bringing in the other states of Europe and then appealing as a united continent for the collaboration of the United States; but irritation at British policy in the Near East combined with the vigorous representations of the American Ambassador to prevent French ratification, and so the Quintuple Treaty and the ulterior design behind it collapsed together. But, though the right to stop and search American ships was unobtainable, the British Government, after long discussion, asserted the right to " visit," without stopping, ships suspected of falsely flying the American flag ; and between 1842 and 1856 many European " slavers " were thus detected and seized. It was a delicate business, however, since the American Government maintained that British officers could make such " visits " only " at their own risk."

The tenacity of the United States on this issue would have mattered much less, of course, if their Government had succeeded in enforcing their own Abolition Laws of 1807 and 1819 with their own navy and police, either on the American or on the African coast. But its efforts in that direction were neither adequate nor continuous. Smuggling slaves from the West Indies into the creeks of Georgia, Florida and Louisiana was still a busy and profitable pursuit long after 1807. One gang at New Orleans made a profit of 65,000 dollars in two years. Smuggling direct from Africa was also undertaken from time to time. And unhappily the American need for slaves continually increased. The development of the cotton-industry demanded more labour than the slave-farms in Virginia or elsewhere could provide : and, when to that was added the burning political question of making new " Slave-States " —which, as it was said by a member of Congress, " cannot be made without Africans "—opinion in the South began to call for the repeal of the anti-Slave Trade Laws. Even Jefferson Davis was opposed to an authorized reopening of the Trade only as a matter of expediency and not on principle. Nor were Americans interested only in the import of slaves into the United States. Those beautiful clippers were built for the general trade with Cuba or Brazil. Rich Portuguese contractors made a regular business of buying and equipping " slavers " in New England ports. Cunha, Reis & Co. of New York was a slave-trading concern. Other joint-stock companies for the promotion of " expeditions to Africa " were formed in New York, Boston and New Orleans. In 1863 the British Consul at New York reported that, of 170 slaving expeditions fitted out between 1857 and 1861, 74 were " known or believed " to have sailed from New York, 43 from other American ports, 40 from Cuba, and the rest from Europe.

Something more than that can be said for the efficacy of American law at the African end of the Trade. The Act of 1819 empowered the President to employ the American Navy for the seizure of American "slavers " on the coast of Africa or elsewhere, and $100,000 were appropriated for the work of suppression. But very few cruisers were sent to Africa and those only at intervals. The appropriation, much of which was spent in providing for freed slaves, sank to $50,000 in 1823 and to $5,000 in 1834 and then to nothing until 1842. In that year, as part of the general settlement of Anglo-American disputes in the

Ashburton Treaty, the United States undertook to co-operate with Britain by maintaining " a sufficient and adequate squadron . . . to carry in all not less than 80 guns . . . for the suppression of the Slave Trade." This agreement was not dishonoured ; for the next fifteen years the average number of American warships assigned to the African service was 4·4 and the average number of guns 77 : but, since the Government set its face against establishing a base for supplies on the coast, most of those vessels' time was spent in voyages to the Cape Verde Islands or Madeira and back. One officer admitted that his ship spent only twenty-two days in fifteen months at its allotted station. Towards the end of the period a more vigorous effort was made. In 1860 President Buchanan obtained an appropriation of $40,000 and dispatched four fast gunboats which made several captures off the Congo. But, broadly speaking, the American Government's effort was far less forcible and far less consistent than its own naval officers would have wished. To them as to their British colleagues it was enough to see the operation of the Trade at close quarters. Their hatred of it was no less fierce. Time and again they boldly broke the rules with which a distant and embarrassed Government had tied their hands in fighting the Trade, and successive British commodores paid warm tributes to their " cordial co-operation."

The result of the United States' refusal to permit the British Navy to give the American flag

a fuller protection from abuse than the American
Navy gave it was a tragic irony—the salvation
of the Slave Trade by the flag of freedom. Most
of the offenders were not Americans. In an inevitable, an almost automatic, sequence the
slave-smugglers of all the world hoisted above
their human cargoes the colours least likely to
be questioned by British cruisers. For the first
twenty years from 1815 it was the Spanish or
French flag they favoured. After the Treaties
of 1833 and 1835 they shifted to the Portuguese,
and after the British Act of 1839 to the only
flag which continued to afford immunity from
search, the Stars and Stripes. Soon after the
passing of the Act the British Ambassador at
Washington reported that " Spanish, Portuguese
and Brazilian slave-traders, with outlaws and
pirates of all nations, are now flocking under
cover of the American flag," and predicted that
" the great bulk of the Trade will soon be carried
on under that protection alone." It was true.
And to make themselves still more secure the
smugglers provided themselves, in case the flag
were questioned, with fraudulent American
papers. Thus American ships were bought by
Spaniards and used for the Cuban Trade under
the pretence of being still American. It became
an open, a notorious scandal. American officials
were well aware of it, but without adequate naval
action they could do little to stop it. Consul
Trist who stamped forged documents at Havana
until he was detected and recalled was happily

an exception. From other consulates came complaints as bitter as Lord Malmesbury's, who spoke of " the atrocious desecration of the American flag." " We are a byword among nations," wrote Consul Wise from Rio de Janeiro in 1843 ; " the only people who can fetch and carry for the Slave Trade without fear of the English cruisers."

Such were the obstacles—the last of them insuperable—that impeded the British effort to stamp out the Slave Trade ; and it is not surprising that, as years went on, as treaty after treaty was laboriously extracted from foreign Governments only to set the smugglers flitting to yet another flag, it began to seem as if Britain was attempting the impossible. What was the use of fishing as long as there were holes in the net ? So far from falling, the estimates of the number of slaves carried over the Atlantic rose. Twenty-five years after the war the annual importation into Brazil and Cuba was reckoned at 100,000 at the least. The total, including Porto Rico, Buenos Aires and the United States, was assessed by some authorities at above 150,000 —a volume which the Trade had never attained even in the busiest years of the eighteenth century. " Twice as many human beings are now its victims as when Wilberforce and Clarkson entered upon their noble task." With that startling challenge Buxton, his long fight with Slavery finished, returned in 1839 to the old battle with the Trade. In *The African Slave*

Trade and its Remedy he set out in full the facts
and figures he had gleaned from official reports,
and urged that the African squadron should immediately be strengthened. But his main point
was that the " strong hand " had so far failed
and would always fail if it was used alone. The
coercive policy should be supplemented by an
attempt to civilize West Africa and especially to
teach its natives how to exploit the wealth of
their own land—an attempt, as he put it, at
" overturning the Slave Trade by civilization,
Christianity and the cultivation of the soil " and
at securing " the deliverance of Africa by calling forth her own resources." In other words,
the " positive policy " of Pitt and Wilberforce.
That policy had long been shelved. The African
Institution, for example, founded to aid in its
pursuit, had been dissolved in 1826. But Buxton's book effectually revived it. Public opinion,
shocked at his figures, rallied to the new call in
the old cause. The African Institution came to
life again as the Society for the Extinction of the
Slave Trade and for the Civilization of Africa,
with Buxton as chairman and a long list of peers
and Members of Parliament, including T. B.
Macaulay, as the Committee. The Melbourne
Ministry, especially Russell and Glenelg, were
not only sympathetic : they took charge of the
movement, and, as a first instalment of Buxton's
ambitious schemes, they organized an official
expedition to ascend the Niger and prepare the
way for commercial enterprise by examining the

economic capacity of the adjacent country and making treaties with its chiefs. In the spring of 1841 the Niger Expedition sailed under the highest auspices. The Prince Consort visited the three steamships in the Thames. Buxton was made a baronet. But the outcome was a tragedy. The ships had hardly entered the river before the fever seized on them. Two of the ships were soon sent back to the open sea, loaded with sick. The third penetrated 320 miles upstream : one treaty was concluded : a model-farm was started : some hasty prospecting was done : and then, with most of her crew out of action, the third ship also was forced to run for safety. Of the 193 white men of the Expedition, 41 died. It was, in fact, a complete fiasco, and it provoked a strong reaction in England. The newspapers fiercely attacked the " fanatics " who had sent their countrymen to certain death. The whole idea of the " positive policy " was dimmed and disparaged. The African Civilization Society, as it had come to be called, was dissolved in 1843. Buxton himself, who had consistently overtaxed his strength, seems never to have recovered from the disappointment. He died in 1845.

The policy of coercion was thus left again to combat the Slave Trade alone : and even that policy at this period was in danger of relaxation, if not abandonment. Buxton, as has been seen, thought it insufficient by itself, but he wished to intensify it, not to give it up. The Abolitionists, however, had remained split into two camps since the later phases of the anti-Slavery campaign : and at the time when Buxton proposed the combination of " positive " with " negative " action, the other wing declared that the latter ought to be dropped altogether. In 1839 the veteran Clarkson republished his *History of the Abolition of the Slave Trade* with a new preface in which it was asserted that, if the Abolition treaties with foreign States did not make it possible to suppress the whole of the Trade at once—as, of course, they did not—they ought to be cancelled, since they " exacerbate the evil a hundred times and are ineffectual to any one purpose but putting money into the pockets of our men-of-war." In the same year Joseph Sturge founded the British and Foreign Anti-Slavery Society which aimed at abolishing Slavery rather than the Trade and on Quaker principles disclaimed the use of force against the latter. These " anti-coercionists " could make a cogent case. Coercion involved the constant harassing, if not bullying, of other nations. It had cost about £15 million since 1815. It consigned British sailors to unhealthy stations. And it had failed. The Trade had not only increased : its cruelties had been intensified, since the fear of cargoes being caught by British cruisers had led to even tighter packing than before. Decks were now often less than three feet apart, sometimes as little as eighteen inches ; and slaves were fitted together " spoon-fashion," so that for days after disembarkation they could not stand upright. Hundreds of slaves, moreover, had been thrown to the sharks to avoid British seizure and condemnation. These were by no means negligible arguments and they were reinforced by those of the Manchester School, now rising to the zenith of its influence in public affairs. British commerce with West Africa was slowly growing. The " Oil-River " traders were finding their feet on the Niger Delta. A substantial, if fluctuating, export of palm-oil was maintained in exchange for British imports. And those imports consisted largely of Manchester cotton-goods. A large part of them unhappily went to meet the needs not of " legitimate " business but of the slave-smugglers who bought them to sell again for slaves, but it cannot be supposed that there were many, if any, merchants capable of deprecating the suppression of the Trade on that account, especially in view of the attitude which Lancashire was soon to adopt on the slavery-issue in the American civil war : and Cobden and Bright, it need hardly be said, took higher ground. The natural growth of the " legitimate " trade, they said, on both sides of the Atlantic was impeded by this costly and futile coercive policy, which kept the West African coast in a state of war and insecurity and irritated and alienated Brazil, " one of our best customers." Our whole commercial system, said Bright, was being put out of gear by " our meddling with this slave question " and by Palmerston's " benevolent crotchet

for patrolling the coasts of Africa and Brazil ";
and he blamed the Government for taking more
interest in the suppression of the Slave Trade
than in cotton. Bright in this mood was not
the Bright of 1861–5, who scouted the " Free
Trade " argument of the Southern States and
denounced their " infernal system " of Slavery.
Nor was Gladstone the Gladstone of Neapolitan
prisons and Bulgarian " atrocities " when, join-
ing in the assault on the treaties and patrols, he
denied that Providence had ordained " that the
Government of one nation shall correct the
morals of another."

There was power, then, in the attack, but the
defenders of coercion had their answer. It was
not our cruisers that obstructed trade on the
African coast, but, as every oil-trader knew,
the incessant warfare in the interior, directly
due to slave-raiding. The additional suffering caused by tighter packing—and that could
be exaggerated—was outweighed by the salvation of the rescued slaves from lifelong endurance of Cuban or Brazilian slavery; and the
" equipment articles " had put a stop to the
drowning of slaves. The Trade, it was true, had
been terribly increased by Europe's demand for
slave-grown sugar and cotton; but nobody had
expected that British " coercion " by itself would
completely extinguish it. We had tried by that
means to reduce it and we had not failed. North
of the Equator the Trade had been confined to
a strip of 300 miles. If the Brazilian Trade, the

most difficult to cope with, kept up its import of slaves at about 20,000 a year, the import into Cuba had been reduced from 25,000 in 1839 to 1,300 in 1845. And, though more had been done to check the Trade by preventing "slavers" from sailing and by seizing them empty than by pursuing and capturing them when loaded, none the less, between 1810 and 1846, more than 116,800 slaves had been caught at sea and freed. In some measure, also, the sufferings of the vastly greater number which were safely smuggled over the ocean had been alleviated; for slaves in Cuba, if not in Brazil, had become more difficult to replace and more expensive and were therefore better treated. So much at least the coercive policy had done, and nothing else could have done it.

The principal defender of the system was its principal author, Palmerston, so often admired or derided as the typical cock-sure, insular, combative "John Bull," but in nothing perhaps more typical of the average Englishman than in his hatred of the Slave Trade. As Foreign Secretary from 1830 to 1841 and from 1846 to 1851 and later as Prime Minister, he was able to operate his coercive policy himself; but he never forgot it, never ceased to keep it before Parliament, when he was out of power. His greatest speech on the theme was made in 1844 when Peel's ministry was confronted with the rising forces of "anti-coercion." It was not a display of rhetorical or dialectical art, nor an

appeal to doctrine or to logic : it was a characteristic attempt to make the House of Commons
see the bare facts of the Trade as he saw them
himself. Taking Buxton's figure for its annual
volume,

Consider [he said] what an enormous mass of
people that represents and what an extent of ground
they would cover. . . . Let anyone imagine that
he saw 150,000 human beings drawn up on a great
plain and that he was told as they marched past
him that they were all travelling to the same doom ;
that this vast living mass of fellow-creatures was
driven on to suffer painful and premature death
under every variety of bodily and mental torture.
Let him further fancy himself told that this was
not a single or an accidental calamity, but that
every succeeding year the same ground would again
be trodden by the same number of victims hurried
forward to the same melancholy fate.

Then, stage by stage, he described the process
of enslavement—the sudden night-raid on an
African village, the huts in flames, the inhabitants rounded up, the healthy men, women and
children picked out and carried off, the aged and
infirm and the infants murdered or left to starve :
the long march to the coast in chains, the weary
and ailing goaded on with the lash till they drop
in their tracks and are abandoned to hunger and
thirst and the beasts of prey : the arrival at the
sea and consignment to the slaver-captain and
another weeding-out of weaklings who are set
adrift on the wild and unknown coast : the

squeezing aboard of the survivors (almost as many have been killed or died by now in the raid or on the march) and the horrors of the "Middle Passage," the cramp and heat and thirst, the filth and smell and disease, the throwing-overboard of any suspected of infectious illness, the ghastly fight for air by the manacled slaves when in rough weather the hatches are closed, death from suffocation, from dysentery, even from fright : and then at last the landing in Cuba or Brazil, the "doctoring up," the sale, the "seasoning" on the plantations, and for those who survive it a life, not often long, of slavery.

Having thus described in cold unsparing detail the actual operation of the Trade and having pointed out that, besides those of its victims who ultimately became slaves, a greater number perished in the process, Palmerston made a straight and simple appeal.

If this has been going on for the last century, how many millions must have been swept away from the population of Africa ! I will venture to say that, if all the other crimes which the human race has committed were added together, they could not exceed the amount of guilt incurred in connexion with this diabolical Slave Trade. Is it not then the duty of every government and of every nation, on whom Providence has bestowed the means of putting an end to this crime, to employ those means to the greatest possible extent ?

Though it meant money out of taxpayers'

pockets and risk of health and life to the seamen on patrol, the average Englishman could only answer that question in one way. And so with most of the political leaders, whether Whig or Tory. If one were to be singled out as second only to Palmerston in the firmness and persistence with which he supported the policy of suppression, it should be Palmerston's own selection, Lord John Russell. When the "anticoercionist" movement reached its full force and threatened for a moment to undermine the Government's resistance, it was Russell who faced it square and broke it. The attack had been opened in the House of Commons in 1845 by Mr. (afterwards Sir) William Hutt, member for Gateshead; he returned to the charge in 1848: and in 1849 he proposed a motion recommending the first steps towards the withdrawal of the patrol. It was rightly suspected that Cobden, Bright and Gladstone would support the motion; and fears were expressed in ministerial circles that, if Russell's Government were obstinate, it might be risking a defeat. So, on the morning of the debate, the Prime Minister called a meeting of his party and told it bluntly that, if the motion were carried, he would resign. The threat did its work. The motion was rejected by 232 votes to 154.

Thus the work of the preventive squadron was continued without a break, and now at last it was nearing its honourable end. Of Cuba and Brazil, who, apart from the smuggling into the

United States, were now almost the only trans-Atlantic importers of slaves, the latter took far the larger number and the patrol of its long coast was more difficult. In 1845, moreover, when the period of the agreement to maintain Mixed Commission Courts came to an end, the Brazilian Government refused to renew it. For some months the Trade ran free, till the British Government made up its mind to treat Brazil as forcibly as its mother-country had been treated in 1839 and carried an Act, known as "Lord Aberdeen's Act," which subjected Brazilian "slavers" to British Admiralty jurisdiction. But any good this Act achieved was more than cancelled by the effect of the British Sugar Act of 1846. The volume of the Brazilian Slave Trade was doubled. In 1849 it was over 50,000. But at this very time a new political party was coming to the front in Brazil, a "national" party, which, increasingly supported by the younger people and armed with a vigorous Press, had set itself in the interests of "pure Brazilians" to break the monopoly of political power which a group of wealthy Portuguese immigrants had hitherto enjoyed. Those Portuguese were the men who ran the Slave Trade : their wealth was drawn from it : and naturally they hated Britain. The "nationalists," it followed, were pro-British and lukewarm, if not hostile, to the Trade. In these circumstances Palmerston felt justified in 1850 in resuming Aberdeen's firm policy. He gave orders that "slavers" should be seized in

Brazilian waters as well as the open sea. There
was uproar at Rio. British residents were in-
sulted. But the big Portuguese business-men
found that they were not strong enough to provoke a general riot ; and after some weeks of
excitement and vacillation the Government sur-
rendered. " I will do all I can to maintain the
honour and dignity of the nation," said the
Foreign Minister, " but you must not suppose
that, when a country like England is in earnest,
you can long maintain a traffic which she is
anxious to suppress." So, for the first time,
firm action was taken to enforce the law. Brazilian cruisers were sent to work with the British.
" Barracoons " on the coast were burned, and
slaves seized as soon as landed. Numbers of
ships were caught. So effective, indeed, was
this swift campaign that the profiteers at Rio,
recognizing that the game was up, fled with their
gains to Portugal. No less than 140 slave-
traders were reported as returning from Brazil
with well over £1 million in their pockets. The
end then came quickly. The number of slaves
imported fell to 3,000 in 1851 and to 700 in 1852.
In 1853 the Trade was said to have stopped.

It remained to deal with the Cuban Trade
which, since Cuba, unlike Brazil, was still a European dependency, was primarily a matter for the
Spanish Government. The Captains-General it
had appointed to govern the island, with one or
two honourable exceptions, had made money by
connivance at the Trade—O'Donnell retired with

£100,000—so that the Abolition of 1820 had been purely nominal. About 1850, unfortunately, the Queen-Mother held a large financial interest in the Trade, and it was largely the operations of her agent that raised its volume in 1853 to 12,500. Sharp remonstrances from the British Government led to attempts to repress the Trade by registration, but these were easily evaded. The patrol of the coast, moreover, was impeded by the fact that American interests were most closely connected with this branch of the Trade ; and when, with the approval of the American Government, the blockade was stiffened, the old controversy over the honour of the Stars and Stripes was inevitably revived. American newspapers, inspired doubtless by the slave-interest, revelled in denunciation of British " outrages " in West Indian waters. Hutt and his friends seized the chance of renewing their agitation against coercion. And in 1858, when Palmerston was out of office, the British Government, more tender towards American feelings than Portuguese or Brazilian, gave orders which meant in practice the surrender of even the right of " visiting " ships flying the American flag. In 1859, accordingly, the number of slaves imported rose to over 30,000. The British patrol on the African coast, however, was maintained, and with the welcome assistance of the four American gunboats it had succeeded by 1860 in almost confining the smugglers to a strip of about 500 miles north and south of the Congo. By these efforts, supplemented by those of a new and honest governor of Cuba, General Serrano, the import was reduced in 1860 to less than 20,000. In 1861 it rose again to 24,000. But that was the last leap of a flickering flame. When Abraham Lincoln took office on March 4, 1861, the Trade was doomed.

Three weeks earlier the long tension between North and South had broken at Fort Sumter. At last it was unnecessary that the humanitarianism of New England, which had never ceased to urge the suppression of the Trade, should be curbed lest it provoke an open schism with the Slave-States. At last the one thing needed for the full and final extinction of the Trade, wholehearted American co-operation, was obtainable.

Lincoln's first blow was the enforcement of the old-standing law. Prosecutions were set on foot at all the ports where the Trade had been established. New York, the blackest spot, was quickly cleansed. The work was done, reported the British consul, with " a vigilance and energy never before witnessed." To prove the Government's earnestness and to serve as a deterrent, one Congo slave-trader, Nathaniel Gordon, was hanged—the first and last culprit to suffer the penalty prescribed by the Act of 1820. The second blow was an Anglo-American treaty. The withdrawal of the American gunboats from the African coast at the outbreak of the Civil War left only one way open by which the pledge to co-operate against the Trade by sea could now be honoured, and a model treaty, conceding the mutual right of search, furnished with the " equipment article," and setting up Mixed Commission Courts, was signed on April 7, 1862, and unanimously ratified by the Senate on April 24. The meaning of this great accord was not mistaken in Madrid. A despatch was sent approving of the measures taken in Cuba by Captain-General Dulce whose *régime* was even stricter than Serrano's. Under these successive strokes the Trade began to wilt away. Deprived of its American bases, it was driven to seek a furtive foothold in European ports, at Marseilles, at Cadiz, even, on one occasion, at Liverpool Deprived likewise of the only flag which had protected it for thirty years, it was more at the mercy of British sea-power than it had ever been. And then, in September 1862, Lincoln's last blow fell. The proclamation that from the beginning of 1863 all slaves in rebel States would be free foretold the end of Slavery, not only in the United States but sooner or later throughout the American world. Already abolished in Uruguay (1842), Argentina (1853) and Peru (1854), it was abolished in Cuba between 1880 and 1886 and in Brazil between 1883 and 1888. With this prospect in view planters were soon abstaining from the purchase of human property that might presently cease to be theirs. The price of slaves at Havana fell steeply. The risks of the Trade became proportionately too great. The Traders began to " shut up shop." The import of slaves into Cuba steadily diminished. In 1865 the British consul was "more than doubtful" whether any slaves at all had been landed. In that year, then, it may be said that the trans-Atlantic Slave Trade came at long last to its end. By a coincidence which recalls the death of Wilberforce in 1833, in that year Palmerston died.

The fact that not Palmerston alone nor Russell but every successive British Government since 1807 had sustained, with little variation of purpose or effort, the fight against the foreign Slave Trade can be simply explained. Though Quaker dislike of force and Cobdenite concern for business and economy had at one time won many votes against coercion in the House of Commons, the great body of the electorate had remained unshaken. "In other countries," said Russell once, "there is no such moral public opinion against the Slave Trade or Slavery." But the average Englishman was unconscious of peculiar virtue. Knowing what the Trade was, he simply thought it so damnable a business that any decent person was obliged to do what he could to stop it.

CHAPTER VII

THE SUPPRESSION OF THE EAST AFRICAN
SLAVE TRADE

THE trans-Atlantic Slave Trade did not draw
the whole of its supply of Negroes from the
west coast of Africa. Slaves were also shipped
from Portuguese East Africa round the Cape to
South America. Though this voyage was more
than half as long again as that from Angola and
though the mortality among the slaves on board
was consequently higher, rising sometimes to half
the cargo, a steady current of traffic was flowing
along this route after the Napoleonic War.
Thus 1,880 slaves from Mozambique were landed
at Rio de Janeiro in 1817, and 2,416 in 1818. Up
to 1825, this branch of the Portuguese Slave Trade,
being south of the Equator and inter-colonial,
was free from interference by British cruisers;
but the establishment of Brazilian independence
and the legislation of 1831 by no means put
an end to it. In 1838 it was reported that about
10,000 slaves a year were being smuggled over
the Atlantic from Mozambique and Quilimane.
In the following decade the activities of the
British patrol substantially decreased the traffic;
but, on the east coast as on the west, smuggling

in greater or less volume continued, under various flags and often with the connivance of Portuguese officials, till the end of Slavery in Cuba and Brazil.

But this was only a fraction of the Trade along the east coast. Unfortunately for the natives of the interior, there were sugar-plantations far nearer than South America. The islands of Bourbon and Mauritius lie only between 400 and 500 miles from Madagascar, and the Mozambique Channel between Madagascar and the mainland is only about 230 miles broad at its narrowest point. Naturally, therefore, the French colonists in Bourbon and Mauritius had been accustomed, long before the Napoleonic War, to obtain their slaves from Madagascar or Mozambique or the Arab coast-towns northwards, and after the war was over they continued to do so. In the case of Bourbon this was not surprising. Captured, like Mauritius, by the British in 1810, it had been restored to France at the peace, and the French Government (as has been seen) made no really effectual attempt to stop the Slave Trade till 1833. French "slavers," therefore, though at least one Governor of the island tried to enforce the law and some few ships were seized, were almost as busy at Bourbon as at Senegal and Goree. More startling, at first sight at any rate, was the continuance of the Trade at the British island of Mauritius. During the first seven years after its capture a great number of slaves, perhaps as many as 30,000, were imported into the island,

and though the traffic decreased in volume after 1817, it was still active till 1821. The Governor of Mauritius from 1812 to 1817 and from 1820 to 1823 was Sir Robert Farquhar, and, though his inertia was severely censured by the philanthropists when the facts came out, there was something to be said in his defence. The colonists he was sent to govern were not Britons, but Frenchmen. Unlike the British planters in the West Indies, they had not been prepared by a long period of controversy for the abolition of the Trade ; and, while the annexation of a foreign colony called for a policy of conciliation towards new and unwilling British subjects, nothing was so likely to antagonize and embitter them as suddenly to destroy a Trade which they regarded as essential to their livelihood and to brand as felons all those of them, including the leaders of society, who were engaged in it. Farquhar, indeed, soon after he took office, went so far as to ask an indignant Colonial Office whether the Abolition Act of 1807 and the penal Act of 1811 applied to a colony which had only been occupied by the British in 1810 and was not yet formally ceded. And when the Acts were duly proclaimed in 1813, he seems to have thought it impossible to enforce them on an island whose creeks and forests made smuggling easy and in defiance of a unanimous local opinion ; it must be admitted, however, that Generals Hall and Darling, who acted in Farquhar's place in 1818 and 1819, succeeded in diminishing the Trade by more open condemnation and more vigorous action, but Darling himself did not minimize the difficulties.

The opulent and powerful part of the Mauritius community [he reported] not only encourage but support the Slave Trade and threaten destruction to those who oppose it. The legal authorities interpose their abilities and professional knowledge to defend the agents of this traffic but not to punish them. The tribunals are as deeply interested in it as any other part of society.

In the light of such facts Farquhar may not have been far wrong in thinking that a more effective and lasting method of abolishing the Trade was to stop it at its export rather than its import end. In pursuit of this policy he negotiated in 1817 a treaty with Radama, the most powerful chief in Madagascar, who had declared himself " King " of the island in 1810, providing for the " entire cessation and extinction " of the Trade throughout his dominions ; and in 1821 he joined with the Government of Bombay in a similar attempt to stop the Arab " slavers " coming from the north.[1]

The continuance of the Trade at Mauritius was not unknown to the British Government. When the Foreign Office pressed at Paris for stricter measures against the Trade, it was humiliating to be told—as the British ambassador was told by the Duc de Richelieu in 1818 —that thousands of slaves were being imported

[1] See p. 197 below.

into a British colony. But Ministers seem to have hesitated to interfere with their " man on the spot," and public opinion was quite in the dark until Buxton, having obtained information from General Hall among others and worked up the case with the aid of the indefatigable Macaulay, startled the House of Commons in 1826 with a full rehearsal of the scandal. The result was an official commission of inquiry which reported that the revelations were substantially true up to 1818 but that since 1821 slave-smuggling into Mauritius had been reduced to very small proportions. Though Buxton was probably right in believing that even after 1826 a little smuggling still went on, it could not, of course, survive the end of Mauritian slavery in 1833.

This Slave Trade to Bourbon and Mauritius was relatively a limited and local affair. Far wider in range and greater in volume was the Arab Slave Trade in the North which for centuries past had been exporting Negroes from mid-Africa northwards by the Nile to Cairo and east and north-east through the Arab coast-towns to Arabia, Persia and India. Little was known of this traffic in England at the outset of the nineteenth century, but the close contact with Egypt occasioned by the Napoleonic War and the growing interest of the Government of British India (administered till 1858 by the East India Company under the supervision and control of the British Government) in the area of the Persian Gulf and in the " overland route " to

Europe through the " Middle East " soon brought the facts to light, and successive British Governments, not content with their efforts to suppress the European Slave Trade, attempted also to combat this far older and more tenacious Arab Slave Trade. The two campaigns were similar in one respect : British ministers were dealing in Egypt, Arabia and Persia as in Europe with independent States, and the political balance of the " Middle East " was so unstable and the importance of maintaining friendly relations along the lines of communication with India so great that it was, on the whole, as difficult to press an Abolition policy on those countries as on France and more difficult than on Spain or Portugal. In a second respect the two problems were quite different. In Europe not only was Slavery now generally regarded as a violation of Christian principles but the Powers to whom the spokesmen of Britain were appealing had solemnly pledged themselves to the abolition of the Slave Trade. In the " Middle East," on the other hand, they were appealing to Moslem rulers who regarded Slavery as a natural and necessary element in their social life, explicitly sanctioned by their religion, and who were as yet incapable of sharing the strange humanitarian sentiment towards the Slave Trade which had so recently grown up in Europe.

There could be little prospect, therefore, of achieving substantial results as quickly in the Asiatic as in the European world ; but in the early days of the Abolition movement a tentative attack was begun. The little Arab State of Oman held one of the key-positions in the naval and commercial strategy of the "Middle East." Its capital, Muscat, commanded the approach to the Persian Gulf into which a large part of the Slave Trade from East Africa was directed. Its rulers, moreover, the Imams of Muscat, claimed, but had not effectively or permanently established, a right of sovereignty over the slave-exporting Arab towns on the East African coast, several of which had been founded long ago by colonists from Oman. In 1812, accordingly, the Government of Bombay, by whom the relations of British India with the "Middle East" were mainly conducted, requested Seyyid Said, a young prince of outstanding ability who had recently usurped the throne of Oman, to do what he could to suppress the trade in slaves from Africa. This gentle pressure was repeated in 1815.

I feel the strongest inducement [wrote Governor Nepean to Said] to recommend to your adoption an example so worthy of imitation as that which the abandonment of this Trade by the principal powers of Europe affords, under an assurance that your acquiescence in this proposition will be extremely gratifying to the British Government.

But Said, of course, did not acquiesce. The motives of the request must have seemed to him almost unintelligible. To yield to it would have excited not only the baffled astonishment but the violent anger of his subjects, especially those engaged in the Trade. He would almost certainly have lost his throne, which like most Arabian thrones was never secure, and probably his life. So nothing happened, and the next move was directed not at Muscat but at the piratic tribes inside the Persian Gulf. In 1819 their long-continued depredations on British shipping were brought to an end at last by a strong military expedition from Bombay, and in the General Treaty of 1820 the chiefs pledged themselves to abstain not only from piracy but also from " the carrying off of slaves from the coasts of Africa or elsewhere." The strict observance of such pledges, however, could not be enforced without a larger naval force than was available in the Indian Ocean, and the Arabs of Oman and the south coast of Arabia continued, free of any pledge, their agelong and profitable pursuit of fetching slaves from East Africa.

Meantime the cruel facts of the Trade were being brought more frequently and directly under British eyes. Cruisers of the Cape squadron, patrolling the coast up to Madagascar and beyond to check the traffic with Mauritius, were often overhauling the Arab sailing-ships in which the slaves were carried under far worse conditions even than those of the Atlantic Trade ; and their captains' reports of what they saw were duly submitted to the Admiralty. Captain Moresby, for instance, wrote as follows :

The Arab *dhows* . . . are large unwieldy open boats without a deck. In these vessels temporary platforms of bamboos are erected, leaving a narrow passage in the centre. The Negroes are then stowed, in the literal sense of the word, in bulk, the first along the floor of the vessel, two adults side by side, with a boy or girl resting between or on them, until the tier is complete. Over them the first platform is laid, supported an inch or two clear of their bodies, when a second tier is stowed, and so on until they reach above the gunwale of the vessel. The voyage, they expect, will not exceed 24 or 48 hours ; but it often happens that a calm or unexpected land-breeze delays their progress. In this case a few hours are sufficient to decide the fate of the cargo. Those of the lower portion of the cargo that die cannot be removed. They remain until the upper part are dead and thrown over. And from a cargo of from 200 to 400 stowed in this way, it has been known that not a dozen at the expiration of ten days have reached Zanzibar.

Such descriptions had a cumulative effect ; and it was with the full concurrence of the Home authorities that in 1821 joint pressure was brought to bear on Said by the Governments of Mauritius and Bombay to enter into an agreement to limit the range of the Trade carried on by his subjects. This time Said was prepared to submit. He resented, no doubt, this unaccountable interference in his affairs as much as his subjects would resent his yielding to it. The proposed limitation, moreover, would entail, so he estimated, a loss of revenue in customs-dues on slaves equivalent to £9,000 a year. But there was no shrewder politician in the " Middle East " than Said. British friendship, backed by British sea-power, had already saved him from his enemies in Arabia. It was his surest safeguard in the uncertain future. To strengthen it, to establish a claim on British gratitude, was worth a sacrifice. He declared, therefore, that, while he could not do all the British wanted—the abolition of Slavery in his dominions and of the " internal " Trade that sustained it was utterly impossible—he was willing to abandon the " external " Trade with foreign States. In 1822, accordingly, he signed a treaty, presented to him by the happy Moresby, in which he undertook to prohibit " all external traffic in slaves " and in particular the sale of slaves to any Christians, to punish any of his subjects who engaged therein, and to permit British cruisers to seize any slave-ship of theirs if found at sea south of Cape Delgado or east of a line drawn from Diu Head to a point sixty miles east of Socotra.

It was potentially a useful treaty, but, like all other Abolition Treaties, it was not easy to enforce ; and, while there is no reason to doubt Said's good faith, it was impossible for him to prevent those little *dhows* from creeping creek by creek along the coast and making a dash, when the wind served, for Mozambique or Bourbon. And when, as it chanced, in 1823 Captain William Fitzwilliam Owen, a high-minded if eccentric man, came sailing up East Africa in command of an Admiralty survey-expedition, he met with all too much evidence that the Moresby Treaty was being violated.

The sequel was a curious incident in the history of the British Empire. Just at the time of Owen's arrival Said was engaged in an attempt to force the Arab coast-towns to recognize his " overlordship." Most of them submitted, but Mombasa, the strongest and most important, clung stubbornly to its independence and appealed to the Government of Bombay to save it from Said's vengeance, offering to submit to British rule in return for the protection of the British flag. Aware that, if this offer were accepted, Said would lose all faith in British friendship and good faith, Governor Elphinstone declined it. But, when the matter came to Owen's ears, he regarded it as a golden opportunity of dealing a blow at " the diabolical traffic in slaves," and he determined to take action on his own account. Putting in at Muscat, he gave Said to understand that, unless he promised to abolish the whole Slave Trade in his dominions, internal as well as external, within three years, he (Owen) would give Mombasa the protection it desired. Said, of course, could make no such promise. All he could do was to dispatch a hasty and vehement protest to Bombay, while Owen sailed off to Mombasa, where he entered into a convention with the Sheikh and the council of chiefs, establishing a British protectorate and—a clause on which Owen laid great stress—abolishing the local Slave Trade. Having hoisted the British flag and left a young lieutenant as " commandant " with a corporal of marines and three seamen in charge of the " protectorate," he proceeded to Mauritius and obtained from Sir Lowry Cole, Farquhar's successor as Governor, a provisional acquiescence in his action, pending a decision by the Government at home. In his report to the Admiralty Owen pleaded earnestly for the maintenance of the " protectorate," pointing out that the territory of Mombasa extended a long way down the coast, that it was strategically and economically valuable, and that—it was on this again he most vigorously insisted—the presence of a British official on the spot was the one certain means of stopping the Slave Trade. " I have taken my own line to the honour of God and my King and to the benefit of my country and of all mankind."

Meantime the Government of Bombay was reporting its opinion on the subject to London. Said, it explained in its final dispatch, had received many assurances of British goodwill and made sacrifices to retain it, especially in connexion with the Moresby Treaty : and, though his legal claim to the overlordship of Mombasa was questionable and though a British occupation of it might assist in the suppression of the Slave Trade, it would be unjust and impolitic to maintain the protectorate without paying Said an indemnity. But before this dispatch was received the British Government had come to its decision. Another naval officer, who had called at Mombasa since Owen's departure, had reported that the Arabs, having forgotten, it seems, their fears of Said, were no longer anxious for a protectorate and were chafing under the restrictions it involved. Bathurst, the Colonial Secretary, accordingly instructed Cole to take " no further measures." But owing to the vagueness of these orders and the difficulty of dealing with the details of the evacuation by long-range correspondence, the little garrison which had been posted at Mombasa in February, 1824, was not withdrawn till July, 1826. For more than two years the British flag had floated over Fort Jesus, and under its shadow no trade in slaves had been permitted.

Twelve years later, the idea of a British occupation of Mombasa was revived. Buxton, convinced that naval patrols were not enough to stop the Trade, suggested that Mombasa might become in British hands a centre of " legitimate " commerce and be used to further the " positive policy " for the suppression of the Trade ; to which Palmerston replied that such a policy would be unavailing unless applied on a vast scale since, " as long as there should remain any great extent of coast unprovided with those commercial settlements, you would not have cured the evil." There was logic, as usual, in Palmerston's case ; but, though the notion of any large-scale British occupation of territory in

East Africa was fantastic in 1838, time was to reveal more than a grain of logic in Buxton's case also. Only by British occupation in the end, and by no other means, was the Arab Slave Trade to be finally abolished.

Palmerston also pointed out that Said was now in full possession of Mombasa and about to conclude a treaty of amity and commerce with Britain. Since Owen's day, in fact, that clever and far-sighted prince had greatly enlarged his power and prestige. Perceiving that East Africa offered an opportunity, denied in dry and rocky Oman, of increasing trade and heightening revenue, he boldly transferred his court to Zanzibar, finally established his political control over all the Arab coast-towns, and set himself to encourage and extend the old caravan-trade with the interior. Led by Arabs or half-Arabs, the caravans began to penetrate to the Great Lakes and beyond—from Mombasa to Victoria Nyanza, from Bagamoyo to Tanganyika, from Kilwa to Nyasa—terrorizing the natives with the guns of their retainers, trading peaceably at times but pillaging and murdering if they chose, and so, after two or three years in the interior, returning to the coast with their loads of ivory and gangs of slaves. The slaves were consigned to Zanzibar or distributed among the coast-towns, which, being " internal " trade, was permitted by the Moresby Treaty but many of them were smuggled in violation of it oversea to Somaliland, Arabia, and Persia. The ivory and other African products were sold, mostly at Zanzibar, in exchange for manufactured goods from India, Europe and America; and to foster this trade Said concluded commercial treaties with the United States in 1833, with Britain in 1839, and with France in 1844, giving facilities for business and providing for the establishment of consulates. Taken as a whole, this economic policy of Said's was a great success. His customs-revenue increased at least eightfold, and Zanzibar became the one great commercial centre in the East African area.

The appointment of Captain Hamerton to reside at Zanzibar in 1841, as political agent for the Government of India and as British consul under the Foreign Office, was not primarily or even largely for the sake of commercial interests —for many years British trade at Zanzibar was meagre and far less than American, French or even German—but on the side of the Indian Government it was mainly to watch over the many British-Indian subjects who migrated to Zanzibar to do business, and on the side of the British Government it was almost wholly to maintain its efforts for the suppression of the Slave Trade. To that end Said was pressed to yield a further step, and in 1845, though his annual revenue from the Trade had increased by then to more than £20,000, he concluded with Hamerton a new treaty prohibiting the export of slaves altogether from his African dominions. This permitted the Trade to con-

tinue between the mainland Arab ports and
between them and Zanzibar, which was essential
for the continuance of Slavery; but it precluded their transportation oversea, even to
Said's own Arabian realm in Oman. Like its
predecessor, however, it was only a treaty; and
a smuggling trade across that corner of the
Indian Ocean was briskly sustained by the fierce
seamen of South Arabia who bore down on
Zanzibar in a cloud of little *dhows* with the southward *monsoon* in December, and, despite all the
few British cruisers could do, collected their
cargoes of slaves and stealthily slipped off home
with the northward *monsoon* in April. The
attempts, similarly, which were made at this
period to stop the smuggling at its import end
—treaties permitting British search and seizure
with the Sheikhs of the Persian Gulf between
1838 and 1847, with the Shah of Persia in 1851,
with the Somali chieftains in 1855 and 1856—
though they served to put some check upon the
Trade, could not avail to stop it altogether.

Matters were made worse at this juncture by
the re-entry of a European Power into the old
game under a new guise. When as a result of
the French Revolution of 1848 Slavery was
abolished in all French colonies, the planters of
Bourbon, now re-named Réunion, found themselves in the same straits for labour as the
planters of Mauritius fifteen years before, and
for a time they tried to meet their needs in the
same way—by importing " coolies " from India.

But the supply obtainable in the French possessions of Pondicherry and Karikal was quite inadequate, and permission to recruit in British India was refused. They had recourse, therefore, to a system known as " The Free Labour Emigration System " which had been in operation on a small scale since 1845. Slaves were bought as of old from the coast-dealers, but now they were set free and invited or told to go and work in Réunion for five years. The system was supervised by French officials and not inhumanely conducted: but, apart from the validity of the contract, it was clear that the Negroes had been obtained in the first instance by the old process of enslavement and that the demand for them would keep up the old bloodshed and disorder in the interior. In fact it intensified it. Arab slave-raiding, especially in the neighbourhood of Lake Nyasa, increased. Ships, full of *émigrés*, were soon leaving the coast for Réunion every few weeks. A business-house in Marseilles contracted to supply the island with 25,000 Negroes within two years. It made no difference to the French Government that Said at Zanzibar or Mejid, who succeeded to the " Sultanate " on Said's death in 1856, protested that they viewed this trade from their " dominions " as a violation of the Hamerton Treaty. Their acquiescence in the " System " was enforced by the dispatch of French cruisers to Zanzibar. In 1854 Portugal was persuaded to permit the traffic within certain

205

limits in Mozambique; and when in 1858 an unusually conscientious Governor-General seized and confiscated the *Charles et George* with over 100 purchased slaves aboard, Napoleon III sent two French battleships to the Tagus to demand the liberation of the vessel and compensation for the outrage. Needless to say, the British Government had protested against the " System " from the outset, firmly declaring that they regarded it as a form of Slave Trade, but the French replied as firmly that it was nothing of the sort. If the blacks were not engaged to work of their free will, said Napoleon in 1859, meeting only half the case, he would not protect a traffic so contrary to progress, humanity and civilization. In 1861, however, the importation of " coolies " from British India was at last conceded by treaty. In 1862 the shipping of Negroes to Réunion ceased. It continued for two more years to the new French settlements on the west coast of Madagascar and in the Comoro Isles, but in 1864 the " System " was finally abolished.

Meantime another great man had appeared on the African stage, a successor to the inheritance of Sharp and Wilberforce and Buxton, who was to work in his way as they had in theirs for the salvation of the Africans.

David Livingstone was born in 1813 at Blantyre of humble Highland stock. Set to work at the age of ten at a cloth factory, he was seized, as he grew older, with the idea of becoming a medical missionary. In the winter of 1836 he began studying at Glasgow University, living on the wages he had earned in the summer. In 1838 he was accepted by the L.M.S., and two years later he obtained his medical degree, was ordained as a missionary, and sailed for South Africa. His first station was at Kuruman in Bechuanaland under Robert Moffat ; but he was too singular a character, too individualist and self-reliant, to settle down to the sedentary life of a missionary settlement, and he was soon away exploring the fringes of the Kalahari Desert and founding new stations, always farther north, till in 1847 he was at Kolobeng, nearly 300 miles from Kuruman. In 1849 he made his first important geographical discovery, pushing with two white companions 800 miles north, at the risk of death by thirst in the desert, to Lake Ngami. It was at about this time that Livingstone had his well-known brush with the neighbouring Boers of the Transvaal who had " trekked " away from Cape Colony, ten years or so before, partly owing to the abolition of Slavery therein,[1] and who undertook in the Sand River Convention of 1852 to abolish it themselves in return for the recognition of their domestic independence. But Livingstone suspected them of indulging in something akin to Slavery and the Slave Trade under cover of obtaining native children as apprentices, and

[1] See p. 150 above.

they suspected Livingstone of encouraging the natives in their hostility and even of supplying them with firearms. But Livingstone had soon left this quarrel far behind him. He was afire now with the idea of cutting a path for Christianity into the inmost core of the " dark interior." " Who will penetrate through Africa ? " he asked. And in 1851 he made his way to Linyanti and the upper reaches of the Zambesi, in the centre of the continent, between Angola and Mozambique. It was there that he first discovered what the Arab Slave Trade meant and how deeply it was now thrusting its fangs into the heart of Africa : and this discovery determined his career. He came at once to the conclusion that the only way really to stop the Slave Trade was to open up the African interior to European commerce and Christianity—in other words, the " positive policy " of Wilberforce and his successors and of the Niger Expedition. But he was not content with projects, like Owen's or Buxton's, for establishing Europeans on the coast. To cut the Trade at its roots he wanted settlements as far inland as conditions of climate and facilities of access would permit—settlements of traders and even, in restricted numbers, of farmers as well as of missionaries. And it was to find out whether a practicable route existed from the sea to the healthy highlands above the Upper Zambesi that he undertook his greatest adventure. Between 1853 and 1856, he made his way, mostly on foot, with only a few native companions, with very little money or goods for barter, without any proper equipment at all, first from Linyanti to S. Paolo de Loanda on the coast of Angola and then back across the continent to Quilimane on the coast of Mozambique. It is claimed that a Portuguese or half-caste trader had wandered from one coast to the other a few years earlier; but, apart from that, this was the first known passage over Africa. Achieved under far harder conditions than those of any later African exploration, it showed that Livingstone possessed an astonishing courage—his friends declared he did not know what fear meant—an indomitable tenacity of purpose and power of endurance, and a remarkable gift for winning the trust and affection of the natives. It also made him suddenly a famous man. On his return home in 1857 the Queen and her ministers, the cities, the universities, the press, all poured their honours on him. He made a triumphant progress through England and Scotland, and wherever he went he pleaded for the rescue of the Africans. On one famous occasion, at Cambridge, he foretold his own death.

I know that in a few years I shall be cut off in that country which is now open; do not let it be shut again. I go back to Africa to try to make an open path for commerce and Christianity. Do you carry out the work which I have begun. I leave it with you.

When he did go back to Africa in 1858, it was

in command of an official expedition which the
Government, in tune with public opinion, had
equipped with the object of exploring the Zambesi and discovering whether steamships could
maintain communication by that route with a
British settlement on the higher lands of what
is now Northern Rhodesia. The "Zambesi
Expedition" lasted nearly six years. In so far
as it had no immediate results—it found the river
blocked by the Kebrabasa rapids and no settlement was attempted—it might have seemed,
like the Niger Expedition, a failure. But in
reality its achievements, direct and indirect,
were considerable. It discovered Lake Nyasa
and the Shiré Highlands : and by a direct chain
of events it led in course of time to the creation
of Nyasaland.[1]

But the most far-reaching result of the Zambesi Expedition was the new impetus it gave
to the revival of the old Abolitionist movement
in England which had done so much to kill the
European Slave Trade and was now to kill the
Arab. In his crossing of Africa Livingstone had
only heard of the Trade. In his wanderings
near Lake Nyasa he saw it—saw it often and
at close quarters, saw the fighting, the bloodshed, the burning villages, the deserted corn,
the corpses floating down the river, the panic-
stricken fugitives, the chained slave-gangs on
their way to the coast. Burning with pity and
aware that the only European Government in

[1] See p. 225 below.

the vicinity could or would do nothing to stop it—some of the Portuguese officials indeed connived at it—Livingstone sought permission from Lord John Russell at the Foreign Office " to take possession of new discoveries as of Her Majesty " as the only means of saving the unhappy people. For that drastic measure British ministers were not yet ready : but Livingstone, when he revisited England in 1864, continued to use all his great influence to keep the new Abolitionist sentiment alive and active. In 1865 he was back in Africa, alone again this time as he preferred to be, making inland up the River Rovuma, becoming more and more convinced as he went on that exploration was the essential prerequisite of " commerce and colonization," and presently obsessed with the idea that somewhere among the Greak Lakes he would discover the source of the Nile. So, year after year, he wandered on and on through the vast trackless country between and beyond Lakes Nyasa and Tanganyika, lost to the outer world till Stanley met him in 1871, but refusing to return to it till his goal was won, gradually failing in health and vigour but never in courage or purpose, till at last, in 1873, near Lake Bangweolo he died. " All I can say in my solitude is," he wrote towards the end in reference to the Slave Trade, " may Heaven's rich blessing come down on anyone—American, English, Turk —who will help to heal this open sore of the world."

When he penned those words, though he could not know it in his distant wilderness, a great step was being taken to alleviate the sore if not yet quite to heal it. The new Abolitionist movement had moved. The growth of the Arab Slave Trade, as revealed by Livingstone, was discussed in Parliament, and successive committees were appointed to report on it. The more evidence was taken, the more the truth stood out that, as long as the Trade was permitted at all, as long as slaves could be bought and sold in the great market at Zanzibar, there would be no end to the slave-raiding in the interior nor to the smuggling of slaves, in violation of the Treaty of 1845, to Arabia and Persia. It was shown, for instance, that of about 20,000 slaves imported into Zanzibar each year, some 16,000 were re-exported, of which only 1,000 were captured and released by British cruisers. And the more the facts were known, the more intolerable to British feelings seemed the continuance of the horrors they portrayed. The following, for example, is a description by a naval officer of what happened to the cargo of a slave-*dhow* stricken by disease :

At the first discovery of small-pox amongst them by the Arabs, all the infected slaves were at once thrown overboard, and this was continued day by day. . . . When they found the disease could not be checked, they simply left them to take their chance and die. Many of the children were of the tenderest years . . . most of them bearing marks of the brutality of the Arabs in half-healed scars and bruises inflicted by lash and stick.

And this is taken from similar accounts of the Zanzibar market :

The market was well on when we arrived. There were perhaps twenty auctioneers, each attending a separate group and selling away as hard as possible. One of the officers counted over 300 slaves present. . . . [One] " lot " appeared to be lately imported ; they were all young boys and girls, some of them mere babies ; and it was amongst them that the terribly painful part of the slave-system was to be seen. . . . The sight is simply horrible, and no amount of sophistry or sentiment will reconcile us to such a condition of things. Skeletons with a diseased skin drawn tightly over them, eyeballs left hideously prominent by the falling away of the surrounding flesh, chests sunk and bent, joints unnaturally swelled and horribly knotty by contrast with the wretched limbs between them. . . . The price of one boy was seven dollars ; he was stripped and examined by a connoisseur, his arms felt, his teeth examined, his eyes looked at, and finally he was rejected. . . . The examination of the women was still more disgusting. . . .

Evidence such as this was more than enough to account for the unanimous recommendation of the Select Committee of 1871, presided over by Mr. Russell Gurney, that the Slave Trade in East Africa should no longer be merely limited but stopped. But it was not easy for the Government to concur. Zanzibar and its dependencies were, after all, an independent sovereign State.

And the attitude of its Sultan, now Seyyid Burghash, to the idea of a complete cessation of the Trade was naturally the same as Said's had been fifty years before. The end of the Trade in Zanzibar, just as much as in the West Indies or Mauritius, meant the end of Slavery. If Burghash conceded it, the loss of his revenue, which would probably amount to £10,000 and possibly to £20,000, would be the least of his troubles. He would be regarded, as Said would have been, as a traitor to his people and their faith and he would incur the violent hostility of everyone engaged in the Trade, especially those fierce and lawless Arabs from the north. It would mean, as it had always meant, a threat not only to his unstable throne but to his life. Under such circumstances to press Burghash too hard might throw him for sheer safety into the arms of France who had long contested British influence at Zanzibar. On the other hand, the lapse of fifty years, which had wrought such changes in Christian Europe, had at least affected the atmosphere of Asiatic and Moslem communities. The long, persistent British assault on the slave-system was now notorious. The thought that Slavery might really come to an end was no longer inconceivable. As against the peculiar difficulties of the situation, moreover, the British Government possessed a peculiar advantage in the personality of its agent on the spot. John Kirk, born at a Scottish manse in 1832, had served on the Zambesi Expedition as botanist and medical officer and proved himself its most hard-headed and trustworthy member after Livingstone himself. The virgin luxuriance of unknown Africa had fascinated his scientific spirit; and the sight of the Slave Trade had fired him with the desire to have a hand in killing it. When, therefore, a subordinate and ill-paid appointment on the staff of the British political agency at Zanzibar fell vacant in 1866, he applied for it and with Livingstone's warm support obtained it. Thus for the next seven years, while he quickly mounted the official ladder—he became Consul-General in 1873—he was working in his island office at the same task as Livingstone, wandering in the wild interior to the westward. And in the course of that work he acquired a unique knowledge not only of the African Slave Trade but of the human and natural history, the peoples and customs, the flora and fauna of the coastland belt. Still more important, his candour, patience and firmness won from the Sultan a trust and respect he gave to no other European. Hence Kirk was able to exercise a quiet constant pressure on Burghash, to convince him that the British Government was in earnest, to promise him at need the protection of British warships against his own turbulent subjects, to persuade him that British friendship, however high its price, was worth more than French.

The climax came in 1873. Spurred on by public opinion—a big meeting of the Anti-

Slavery Society was held at the Mansion House in 1872—the Government dispatched Sir Bartle Frere, lately Governor of Bombay, on a special mission to obtain the Sultan's acquiescence in a treaty finally and completely abolishing the Trade throughout his dominions and prescribing the closure of the slave-markets. For a whole month Frere and Kirk argued with Burghash and his councillors. At times the Sultan wavered, but in the end he listened to less disinterested advisers and refused to sign the treaty. To give him time to change his mind Frere left Zanzibar for a month's cruise along the coast. On his return the answer was the same. Then the mission finally sailed away, but, when it touched at Mombasa, Frere sent back instructions to Kirk to give the Sultan one last warning and, if it failed, to co-operate with the British naval officers at Zanzibar in taking charge of the customs-house and stopping the Trade by force. Frere took this action on his own responsibility, and, when his report of it reached London, there was agitation in the Cabinet till Ministers remembered that Palmerston had done much the same thing in Brazil in 1850 and with the best results. Meantime the best results had accrued at Zanzibar. Probably no other man than Kirk could have handled such diplomatic gunpowder without an explosion. As it was, the Sultan yielded : his councillors sullenly acquiesced : on June 5, five weeks after Livingstone's lonely death 700 miles away, the Treaty was signed by

Burghash and Kirk : and almost before the ink had dried, messengers were sent to close the gates of the old slave-market for ever. And this was all achieved without straining, much less breaking, the Sultan's attachment to Kirk and his country. Two years later, at his own strong wish, Burghash paid a friendly visit to England, and was received by the Queen at Windsor. As he observed the proofs on every hand of a wealth and power far beyond all his previous conceptions, he confessed his surprise at the patience and gentleness with which the British Government had treated him. "Why didn't you knock me on the head," he asked, "when I first refused to sign the Treaty ? "

The Treaty of 1873 was the death-warrant of the Arab Slave Trade which had preyed for so many centuries on East Africa. On the site of the Zanzibar slave-market a cathedral church was built by the Universities' Mission, its altar standing where the whipping-post had stood. But, as Kirk had prophesied, the Trade still took some time in dying. As long as Slavery existed in the Zanzibar dominions and in the Asiatic countries just across that corner of the Indian Ocean, so long a trickle of smuggling still evaded the British cruisers. In 1876 Burghash, after friendly consultation with Kirk but on his own initiative and without external pressure, not only prohibited the fitting out of slave-caravans on the coast, denied them access to it from the interior, and vetoed the transport of slaves from port to port along it under pain of confiscation, but also abolished the legal status of Slavery itself in the northern part of his dominions. Even this drastic action was not conclusive. Smuggling still continued across the narrow channel from the mainland to the islands of Zanzibar and Pemba : and it was only finally stamped out when the Trade was stopped at its source by the British and German occupation of the interior after 1889 and at its terminus by the "outlawing" of Slavery in Zanzibar, by then a British Protectorate, in 1897. At the end of the century at last the Arab Slave Trade in East Africa was dead.

CHAPTER VIII

THE LAST PHASE

THE ultimate lesson of the long fight with the Arab Slave Trade in East Africa was that it could not be completely suppressed by treaties and patrols at sea, nor even by European occupation of the coast-ports. For its complete suppression one of two alternatives was needed : the cessation of the demand for slaves at the import-end (which was what had finally killed the Atlantic Slave Trade) or the stopping of it at its main source of supply in the heart of Africa.

As regards the first alternative, the demand for slaves continued throughout the nineteenth century, and still in some degree continues, in Africa itself and in Asia. (1) In Africa the Slave Trade was still in 1880 and later supplying furtively or openly the needs of the Moslem communities in North Africa from Egypt to Morocco, of the Moslem Emirates in Northern Nigeria, of Abyssinia, and of the islands of Madagascar, Zanzibar and Pemba. Round the Great Lakes, moreover, and in the Congo country, powerful Arab traders or adventurers were still seizing slaves for their own local use as well as for export. And to that may be added, though it does not belong to the Slave Trade in its usual sense, the continued enslavement of fellow-Africans by strong and warlike tribes, especially in West Africa, where it was associated with the hideous practice of human sacrifice. (2) In Asia the demand for African slaves was confined by 1880 to the " Middle East." All import of slaves into British India had been prohibited by the Company's Government in 1811, and the Charter Act of 1833, passed when the question was in the forefront of British politics and the younger Grant was President of the Board of Control, prescribed that Slavery should be brought to an end as soon as possible. Wholesale abolition on the West Indian plan was impracticable in face of Hindu custom as well as Moslem law ; but the same result was equitably and harmoniously achieved by an Act of the Indian Government in 1843 which abolished the legal status of Slavery in British India. That meant the removal of all distinction between slave and free in the eyes of the law : it meant, for example, that no right of property in a slave could be enforced in the courts and that a slave could leave his master whenever he chose without any formal act of liberation. As a result the institution, which had never been an indispensable element in Indian society, rapidly died out. In the penal code of 1860 it was possible to make it a criminal offence to own as well as to trade in slaves. And in course of time, as the force of this example in British India operated on the Native States not amenable to British law, the whole sub-continent was freed from the slave-system. Farther east, the legal status had been similarly abolished in the British settlements in Malaya in 1843 and in Ceylon and Hong-Kong in 1844. But nearer home, in the Moslem world of the "Middle East" (specially in Arabia, where, except in the British Protectorate of Aden, it is still a general and legal institution), Slavery still exists to-day. Over those countries the British Government could not exercise the power or the influence it exercised in India, and into those countries, therefore, the African Slave Trade, though obstructed and confined on the East Coast, still poured its victims from the Sudan and the Lakes by way of the Nile and Cairo or across the Red Sea.

Such was the position when in the course of the 'eighties the European Powers engaged in a sudden and sweeping series of territorial annexations in Africa. This "Scramble for Africa" was conducted at high speed and—a remarkable achievement—without precipitating a European war, so that by the end of the century almost all Africa except Morocco, Tripoli, Liberia, Abyssinia and the Sudan had been officially "partitioned" and subjected in varying measure to the occupation or protection of Britain, France, Germany, Italy, Belgium, and Portugal. The whole problem of the Slave Trade and Slavery in Africa was thus transformed. The Powers still could not stop the demand for slaves in Asia : they

could not occupy and control the whole of the
" Middle East " : but they could stop the demand in Africa through their occupation or control of Tunis, Egypt, Northern Nigeria, the East
African coast, Zanzibar and Madagascar : and
they could stop the supply of slaves at its source
by their occupation of all the slave-country
round the Great Lakes and ultimately of its
northern extension, the Sudan, as well. But
that is not to say that the destruction of the
slave-system was the only or even the dominant
motive of the new " imperialism " in Africa.
Of course there were other and usually stronger
motives. Industrialized Europe had awakened
to the need of African raw materials for her consumption and manufacture and of African markets for her exports. French expansion was also
stimulated by the prospect of obtaining compensation in an African empire for the loss of
Alsace-Lorraine. In Germany and Italy, newly
united nations, there was a body of opinion
which demanded the possession of colonies as a
mark of their national status and an outlet for
their national energies. The British Government had a special interest in safeguarding the
area of the Suez Canal, and in more than one
quarter it was compelled to occupy territory,
which hitherto it had studiously forsworn, for
the simple reason that, if it did not occupy it, a
rival Government would. These were all potent
influences ; but it would be quite untrue to suppose that the humanitarian motive—the idea,

conceived in their different days and ways by Sharp, Wilberforce, Owen, Buxton, and Livingstone, that European occupation of Africa could and should benefit the Africans—was not also at work, though it sometimes figured more prominently in public professions than in fact. Despite its tragic sequel there was a genuine element of philanthropy in King Leopold's institution of the International African Association in 1876 for exploring and civilizing Africa and putting down the Slave Trade, in the appointment of H. M. Stanley to open up the Congo area in 1879, and in the creation in 1885 of the Congo Free State which became the Belgian Congo under happier auspices in 1908. Cardinal Lavigerie, again, though he did not forget the claims of his country and his Church, was more sincere than practical when he preached a " holy war " against Islam and the Slave Trade in Africa in 1888 ; and the real response it evoked among German Catholics gave Bismarck a telling argument on behalf of his colonial policy in East Africa.

But the clearest evidence of the fact that in slicing up the soil of Africa Europe had not entirely ignored the interests of its native occupants is to be found in the Brussels Conference of 1889. The previous Berlin Conference of 1885 had been more or less limited to political and commercial questions within the " Congo Zone," and the Berlin Act in two of its thirty-eight Articles had only committed the Governments concerned " to help in suppressing Slavery and the Slave Trade " within that area. But the object of the Brussels Conference, convened by King Leopold at the British Government's suggestion, was solely humanitarian : it was to aim at " putting an end to the crimes and devastations engendered by the traffic in African slaves, protecting effectively the aboriginal populations of Africa, and insuring for that vast continent the benefits of peace and civilization." Seventeen States took part in it. Besides all Europe, the United States, the Turkish Empire, Persia and Zanzibar were represented. The Conference resulted in a General Act, signed in 1890 and ratified in 1892, in which all the participating States bound themselves, as far as lay within their power, to suppress what remained of the African Slave Trade by controlling the areas in which it originated and setting up efficient administrations therein, by intercepting and liberating gangs of slaves on the march, by the final eradication of the traffic by sea, and by forbidding the import of slaves into territories where Slavery was still tolerated. The Act further prescribed that within a fixed mid-African zone the importation of firearms and of alcohol should be either prohibited or restricted and regulated. This Act has been called " the Magna Charta of the African slave " ; and when, after many months of detailed discussion and keen dispute, the rivalries and jealousies of the leading nations were at last composed, the credit of it was mainly due to Sir John Kirk, recently retired from his twenty-years service at Zanzibar and one of the two British plenipotentiaries at Brussels; for Kirk was not only a very shrewd diplomatist but he knew more about the African Slave Trade than anyone else alive.

It remains to describe the share taken by Britain in the " Scramble for Africa," to explain how far it was inspired by the old Abolitionist tradition, and to show how it resulted in the execution of the mandate undertaken in the Brussels Act.

The first British occupation of the mid-African interior was the direct outcome of Livingstone's appeal for a British commercial and missionary settlement in order to stop the ravages of the Slave Trade in the Lake Nyasa country which he had discovered in 1859. The immediate result of that appeal was the creation of the Universities' Mission to Central Africa which, after an attempt to settle in the Shiré Highlands in 1862 had been tragically thwarted by the prevalence of slave-raiding, retired to a base at Zanzibar whence it gradually pushed its stations inland until in 1882 they reached Lake Nyasa. Meantime the news of Livingstone's death in 1873 had profoundly affected public opinion and led to a new outburst of missionary activity. In 1874 the Livingstonia Free Church Mission was founded in Scotland, and in the following year its pioneers succeeded in floating a small steamship, carried up in sections, on Lake Nyasa. In 1876 the Church of Scot-

H

land mission was established in the Shiré highlands at Blantyre. In 1878 the African Lakes Company was founded, and by 1885 it had not only occupied the shores of Lake Nyasa but had succeeded in making contact with the missionary stations recently established, on Lake Tanganyika and a road was projected to unite the two lakes. It might well have seemed as if this network of "unofficial" enterprise would soon realize Livingstone's dream of blocking the Slave Trade in Nyasaland by planting "civilization, commerce and Christianity" across its path. One of the main tracks of the Trade ran straight through the area of these operations. Groups of slaves, brought partly from the country now known as Northern Rhodesia and partly from the district of the Upper Congo in the north-west, met on the west side of Lake Nyasa, were ferried across in *dhows*, and were thence driven to the sea.

Of the danger threatening them the slave-traders were well aware, and they were by no means ill-equipped to resist it. Since the time of Seyyid Said these Arab or half-breed adventurers had penetrated deeper and deeper inland. Some of them had established a permanent settlement at Tabora, a meeting-place of trade-routes between Lake Tanganyika and the sea. Others, wandering farther afield, had forcibly imposed their rulership on native tribes and used them to fight and enslave their neighbours. Between 1880 and 1890 these lawless and well-armed despots, who had long ceased to render more than a nominal allegiance to the Sultan of Zanzibar and were in any case too far inland to be controlled from the coast, had become the virtual rulers of large areas between the Sudan, the Congo, and the Zambesi. West of Lake Tanganyika the most powerful of them was Tippoo Tib, well known to Livingstone and Stanley, and at the north end of Lake Nyasa, Mlozi. In 1888 the latter, who had declared himself " Sultan of Nkonde," called on the British settlers to recognize his authority and pay him tribute : and on their refusal he prepared to attack them and drive them from the country. It was a perilous situation for the handful of white men involved. A British Consulate for Nyasaland had been established at Blantyre in 1883, but that implied no obligation on the British Government's part to protect the missionaries and traders who had ventured so far from the coast in pursuit of their private ends. All the Lakes Company could do was to arm and organize its white *employees* and such friendly natives as were not afraid to fight for them, and to offer a desperate resistance to the imminent attack.

At this crisis another of the leading figures in the story of this book appears on the stage. Captain Frederick Dealtry Lugard, born at Madras in 1858, after service in Afghanistan, the Sudan and Burma, had been put on half-pay on medical grounds early in 1888, and in the same

year he visited East Africa in search of health
and adventure. On hearing at Zanzibar of the
trouble in Nyasaland, he made his way to Blantyre, learning as he went, like Livingstone and
Kirk before him, about the horrors of the Slave
Trade and the strength of the Arab traders.
Some of them, he was told, could put 5,000
rifles in the field ; and, if common interests and
a common faith should link them with their
fellow-magnates to the north-west and with warlike tribes like the Yao which had been converted
to Islam, something akin to a Moslem dominion
might be created over all the area of the Great
Lakes between the Nile and the Zambesi, a
dominion which, however loosely consolidated,
might be difficult to break. When, therefore,
Lugard was pressed to take command of the Company's forces with the concurrence of the British
Vice-Consul and the Missions, he at once accepted,
and proceeded to Karonga's, the Company's post
near the north end of the Lake where the handful
of men left after the gallant defence of Consul
Hawes and later Consul O'Neill were still holding
their own under promise of help. Lugard's
inspiring personality, his energy and resource,
and the example of his personal courage—he was
seriously wounded in leading an attack on an
Arab stockade—put new heart into the little
garrison ; and, after ten months of fighting with
sickness in the camp as well as the enemy outside it, he had not only held the post but by
taking the offensive had taught the slave-traders

that the expulsion of the British was not the easy task they had imagined. By the spring of 1889 it seemed safe for him to leave Karonga's in order to hasten the supply of arms and ammunition, to ask for diplomatic assistance at Zanzibar, and to plead with the Government and public opinion in England " to save Nyasaland from becoming a Mahomedan Empire with slave-raiders for kings."

A few months later the issue was brought to a head by the action of the Portuguese who, though they had never penetrated, still less occupied Nyasaland, claimed its possession as part of Mozambique and dispatched a military force up the River Shiré. However reluctant the British Government might be to undertake new responsibilities in the African interior, it could not acquiesce in the surrender of the country which Livingstone had discovered to a colonial government whose inefficiency and corruption he had revealed. In 1891 Portugal was compelled to accept a delimitation Treaty, and a British Protectorate over Nyasaland was proclaimed. From that moment the suppression of the Slave Trade was only a matter of time. In co-operation with the British South Africa Company, which under the authority of its charter and the leadership of Cecil Rhodes was now occupying Northern Rhodesia, Sir Harry Johnston, Commissioner of the Protectorate, conducted a campaign against the Traders with Sikh and native troops which culminated in 1895 in their final defeat and dispersion and the capture and execution of their most formidable leader, Mlozi. In 1898, a hundred miles to the west of Lake Nyasa, the last slave-gang in this long tormented quarter of mid-Africa was caught on the march and freed.

Similar developments were occurring, meantime, in the adjacent country to the north. In 1889 the German Government proclaimed a protectorate over the southern half of the Sultan of Zanzibar's mainland dominions (now the British mandated territory of Tanganyika), and, though hampered by an Arab and later by a native rising, it set itself in due course effectively and completely to stamp out the Slave Trade. The northern half of the Sultan's dominions (now known as Kenya Colony and Protectorate) had been acknowledged by Germany in 1886 to be a British " sphere of influence " ; but in view of the repeated refusals of the British Government to undertake its occupation and administration this area would probably have been divided up between other European Powers if the Imperial British East Africa Company had not been formed in 1888 to do what the British South Africa and Royal Niger Companies were doing in other parts of Africa. The B.E.A. Company, like its colleagues, was a business affair, but the difficulties and risks of its task were greater, its hope of earning dividends for its shareholders more remote, and it was more definitely and immediately affected by philanthropic motives. Sir John Kirk and Sir Thomas Fowell Buxton,

grandson of the Emancipator, were among its
founders and directors ; and by Article X of its
charter it bound itself to abolish as far as practicable " any system of slade-trade or domestic
servitude " within its territories.

The promise was not easy to fulfil. The
coastal belt could be controlled from its ports, but
the more thickly-populated area lay far inland
round the shores of Lake Victoria, and in 1888
this country of Uganda was in dire straits.
The introduction of Christianity had led to bitter
strife between Protestant and Catholic con-
verts and between them and the Moslems.
A dangerous body of Sudanese troops, cut
off by the rise of the Mahdi from their pay-
masters in Egypt, was established in the west.
The murder of Bishop Hannington in 1885 had
revealed the hostility of the brutal and cunning
King Mwanga to European intrusion, and the
prospects of British occupation were still further
clouded by the passage through Uganda of a
German expedition under Karl Peters and by the
steady progress of Belgian and French missions
from the Congo and Ubangi towards the upper
waters of the Nile. But of all difficulties the
greatest was that of communication with Uganda
from the coast across 800 miles of country, still
virtually unexplored, covered in parts with thick
bush or jungle, and occupied by such militant
tribes as the Masai. It was Lugard again who
saved the situation. At the instance of Sir John
Kirk, whose close friend and disciple he became

he had returned to East Africa, and towards the end of 1890 he was ordered to take charge of the Company's administration in Uganda. Proceeding by forced marches from Mombasa with a small force of Sudanese and Zanzibaris, he boldly established himself in a fortified camp at Kampala in the centre of Mwanga's capital. It was a critical position, but Lugard's coolness and tact prevailed; and in eighteen months he had succeeded in penetrating and surveying the country as far as Lake Albert, in locating and re-organizing the leaderless Sudanese, in effecting a *modus vivendi* between the Catholic and Protestant factions whose antagonism had culminated in open war, in obtaining a reasonable settlement for the Moslem minority, and finally in winning the confidence of Mwanga and some of his councillors and their acceptance of the Company's flag. But, in the meantime, the Company, having almost exhausted its capital, had reluctantly decided to evacuate Uganda. It seemed, indeed, as if all Lugard's work had been wasted; but he hurried back to England and in a series of public speeches appealed to the British people not to evade or leave to others the task of saving Uganda from the old *régime* of bloodshed and slave-raiding. The missionary societies took up the cry. And at last the Government's opposition to yet another imperialist adventure was shaken. Under strong pressure from Lord Rosebery and not without a sharp dispute in the Cabinet, it consented to send out an official commission of

inquiry. The result was the same as in Nyasaland—the declaration of a British Protectorate
in 1895, the setting up of British administration,
and the final suppression of civil warfare and
the Slave Trade.

So far, so good ; but next to Uganda on its
northern and north-western side lay the richest
of all the " sources " of the Trade. From time
immemorial a steady stream of slaves seized from
among the primitive Sudanese tribes among the
upper reaches of the Nile had flowed northwards by the river to Cairo or across the desert
to the Red Sea and thence over to Arabia. The
establishment of a relatively efficient government
in Egypt in the first half of the nineteenth century had not lessened the evil. On the contrary,
Mahomet Ali, despite the constant protests of
the British Foreign Office, had increased for a
time the previous demand for slaves by trying to
create a great black army to serve his aggressive
designs on the Turkish Empire. Slave-hunts
were conducted by his Egyptian troops. Multitudes of " recruits " were packed off northwards
and drilled and disciplined. Their only failing
was an inability to endure the change of climate
and conditions. " They died like sheep with the
rot." So the scheme was dropped, and the Trade
resumed its normal flow. Regular raids on the
pagan tribes were organized by the fierce Moslem
rulers of the Upper Sudan. Slave-caravans con-
verged on the central halting-place at Khartum.
The number consigned thence to Arabia is un-

known. The annual intake at Cairo was probably about 4,000, of whom some remained with Egyptian masters and some were drafted on to Turkey. After 1830, when the demand for Negroes at Constantinople had been stimulated by the Russian occupation of the sources of slave-supply in Georgia and Circassia, the business and the wealth of the Cairo dealers grew, until, as at Rio de Janeiro, the commercial aristocracy of the country was mainly fed by the Slave Trade. So matters rested till the accession of Ismail Pasha in 1863.

Ismail has been lavishly abused for the recklessness of his financial extravagance and his territorial ambitions, but at least he deserves the credit of having been the first ruler of Egypt who honestly tried to stop the Slave Trade. In 1869 he appointed an Englishman, Sir Samuel Baker, who had proved his courage and force of character in his exploration of the Upper Nile and discovery of Lake Albert, as Governor of the Southern Sudan with instructions to extend the Egyptian frontier southwards and suppress the Slave Trade. It was a superhuman task. The Egyptian troops were unreliable. The Egyptian officials were hand in glove with the slave traders. It is not surprising that Baker resigned in despair in 1873. But Ismail persisted, and in 1874 he chose as Baker's successor a Scot who was probably more capable than any other living man of achieving the impossible in the Sudan. Colonel Charles George Gordon, born at Woolwich in 1833, had served in the Crimea and proved himself an efficient officer of engineers and no more till, having volunteered for service in China and having been lent to the Chinese Government, he suddenly leapt into fame as "Chinese Gordon," the commander of the "Ever Victorious Army" and the saviour of the Manchu Empire from disruption. The sources of his unusual power in will and deed were akin to those of Livingstone's. He likewise did not know what fear meant: he likewise was inspired, day in, day out, by an unflinching, almost a fatalistic faith in the guidance of God. With characteristic energy he threw himself at his task. Reckless of danger and disease and the extreme hardships of travel in the Upper Sudan, with only three or four loyal European subordinates to help him, he penetrated the haunts of the slave traders, broke up their caravans, fought them when he was forced to fight, and pushed his way through to the Great Lakes, believing like other champions of the cause that the surest way to kill the Trade was to open a "highway for civilization" through mid-Africa. And, as with others again, the actual sight of the Trade deepened almost to passion his loathing of it.

You can scarcely conceive [he wrote] the misery of these poor slaves. . . . No one who has a mother or sisters or children could be callous to the intense human suffering which these poor wretches undergo. . . . I declare, if I could stop this traffic, I would willingly be shot this night.

In 1877—the year in which Ismail signed a convention with Britain for the suppression of the Trade and followed it up with measures prohibiting all sale of slaves in Egypt at the end of ten years, forbidding the transport of slaves across Egyptian territory, and establishing a preventive squadron under a British naval officer in the Red Sea—Gordon was raised to the Governor-Generalship of the Sudan, with his headquarters at Khartum and with the Equatorial and Red Sea Provinces added to his charge. The reorganization of so vast an area required a large and well-disciplined army, a host of honest officials, and the backing of a full treasury at Cairo. Gordon had none of these things : but still he laboured on till in 1879, after more than five years of increasing strain, even his iron physique began to fail him. When, therefore, in that year the remnants of the Slave Trade seemed to have yielded to a series of hard blows and when at the same time Ismail, overwhelmed in the wreck of his finances, was deposed, he resigned his charge. Not long after, he heard the bitter news that the new Khedive, Tewfik, had appointed as his successor an Egyptian pasha whom he had himself dismissed for cruelty. His work, it seemed, would soon be undone.

The sequel is familiar history. Egypt drifted rapidly into revolution, and in 1882 the British Government occupied the country with the object of restoring " peace and order." But it did not regard it as part of its duty to maintain the far-flung dominions which Ismail had claimed to rule beyond the old Egyptian frontier. It was decided, therefore, not to resist the Mahdi's rebellion, but to withdraw the Egyptian garrisons from the Sudan. That was Gordon's last task. Surrounded by the Mahdi's fanatical warriors, he was killed in the storming of Khartum on January 26, 1885. The British force, which had been sent to relieve him and arrived just too late, was thereupon recalled, and the Sudan abandoned to dervish rule. It was an appalling fate for the Sudanese. The story of the Mahdi's rule and that of the Khalifa who succeeded him on his death in 1885 is an unbroken record of warfare, massacre, devastation, and famine. Millions of Sudanese died. The inevitable recovery of the Slave Trade was now their least infliction, but that was bad enough. Slatin Pasha, one of Gordon's old lieutenants and a prisoner in the Khalifa's hands, thus described a part of it :

After the defeat of the Shilluks, Zeki Tummal packed thousands of these wretched creatures into the small barges used for the transport of his troops and dispatched them to Omdurman. Hundreds died from suffocation and overcrowding on the journey ; and on the arrival of the remnant, the Khalifa appropriated most of the young men as recruits for his bodyguard, whilst the women and young girls were sold by public auction which lasted several days. . . . Hundreds fell ill ; and for these poor wretches it was impossible to find purchasers. Wearily they dragged their bodies to the river bank where they died; and as nobody would take the trouble to bury them, the corpses were pushed into the river and swept away.

But before the end of the century the agony of the Sudan was ended. The sense of insecurity in Egypt as long as the Khalifa remained master of the Upper Nile, the spread of information as to the character of his rule, bitter memories of Gordon's death—these were among the factors which determined the southward advance of an Anglo-Egyptian army in 1896. In 1898 Kitchener decisively defeated the dervish forces, between forty and fifty thousand strong, at Omdurman: a few weeks later the fugitive Khalifa was caught and killed in battle; and by the end of the year the Sudan had passed under the joint control of the British and Egyptian Governments. Then at last could be done what Gordon could not do. The Egyptian troops had now been disciplined under British officers, the higher officials were now British, and the economic prosperity and financial strength of Egypt had wonderfully recovered under British supervision. The impossible task was now possible. Except for occasional raids from the mountain fastnesses of Abyssinia and occasional smuggling ventures across the Red Sea, the Slave Trade in the area of the Upper Nile was abolished.

Thus, one by one, the sources of the Trade round the Great Lakes on south and east and north, had been occupied and sterilized by 1900

—Northern Rhodesia, Nyasaland, East Africa, Uganda, the Sudan. And the west side had been or was rapidly being dealt with by Stanley and his Belgian successors on the Upper Congo and by the French advance south-east from the Sahara and north-east from Gabon to the Sudanese frontier. It only remained to eradicate that inland native Slave Trade in West Africa which had survived the abolition of the European traffic oversea.

The British share therein was mainly confined to two territories—the Gold Coast and Nigeria. As late as the 1860's there had been little to suggest in either of these areas that a British occupation of any extensive or lasting kind was impending. The old Slave Trade posts on the Gold Coast were struggling to maintain a " legitimate " trade under a British Protectorate. In Nigeria British merchants, inspired by the enterprise and enthusiasm of Macgregor Laird, were similarly engaged on the banks of the Niger ; but the only soil in official British occupation was the little island of Lagos, annexed in 1861 solely because annexation had been shown to be the only means of stamping out the slave-smuggling which infested the creeks and lagoons of the neighbourhood. It was an incident in the fight with the trans-Atlantic Trade, and, when that fight was over, a substantial body of British opinion, oblivious of the " positive policy " of the old humanitarians, took the view that there was no longer any valid reason for maintaining a connexion with West Africa which had cost the British taxpayer at least as much as it had benefited British trade. Thus in 1865 a Select Committee of the House of Commons reported that " all further extension of territory or assumption of government . . . would be inexpedient " and looked forward to " our ultimate withdrawal " from all administration of the West Coast except at Sierra Leone. Nothing, however, was done, and thirty years later the whole situation had been transformed. Trade had rapidly developed. The Gold Coast Protectorate had been extended and reorganized. The Niger merchants, who received a charter as the Royal Niger Company in 1886, had pushed their " sphere of influence " far up the river. And finally, in West Africa as in East, the results of the " Scramble "— mainly in this case the " squeezing " exerted by the French from both sides of both areas— compelled the British Government to consolidate and regularize its position. By 1900, under treaties with France, the boundaries of British rule over the Gold Coast and its hinterland and over North and South Nigeria had been fixed where, with relatively small extensions under " mandate," they stand to-day.

Here as elsewhere, it would be difficult to disentangle the mixed motives of territorial expansion and to ascribe to each its relative weight. There was a clause stipulating for the suppression of the Slave Trade in the Niger Company's charter, and certainly among the motives, felt perhaps more keenly by the officers and men on the spot than by far-away politicians or business men, was the thought that the British flag would save the Africans from barbarous misrule and, in particular in certain areas, from the peculiar atrocity of human sacrifice. The kings of Ashanti, for example, or of Benin were always slave-hunting among the neighbouring tribes in order to provide a hecatomb of victims for their savage idols. The expedition, which was sent to Benin in 1897, found " the City of Blood " had not belied its name : it was strewn with crucified and decapitated corpses. More normal in character, less horrible in its purpose, but much more difficult to cope with was the Slave Trade carried on to meet the usual needs of Moslem society by the emirs and sultans of Northern Nigeria. These were no primitive savage chiefs, but rulers of relatively civilized States, upholders of Islam and Islamic law, and commanders of a formidable cavalry with which at regular intervals they swept southwards across the Niger or eastwards towards the North Cameroons to replenish their supply of slaves. Slave-raiding, indeed, was not only a social necessity : it was an habitual exercise or recreation, a kind of sport. " Can you stop a cat from mousing ? " said the Emir of Kontagora to a British official. " When I die, I shall be found with a slave in my mouth." For such a state of affairs the only remedy was European intervention, and

the thought of ending it was at least a supplementary motive in the extension of British control over Northern Nigeria.

Lugard again was its chief instrument. His
work in East Africa done, he had transferred
his services to the Niger Company, and in 1894
by a notable forced march through unknown
country from Jebba to Nikki he had anticipated
a French intrusion in the north-west corner of
the British " sphere." In 1897, while the Company's constabulary under the direction of Sir
George Taubman Goldie, Governor of the Company, were engaged with the slave-raiding Emirs
of Nupe and Ilorin, Lugard was again sent out
to raise a new body of native troops, the West
African Frontier Force, and in 1900, when the
British Government took over the work of
administration from the Company, he was
appointed High Commissioner of the Northern
Nigeria Protectorate. His immediate task was
to come to terms with the proud and powerful
Moslem rulers of Hausaland and Bornu between
the Upper Niger and Lake Chad, and in less
than three years he achieved it with remarkably
little bloodshed by a combination of soldiership
and statesmanship. Early in 1903 all the princes
had accepted British " protection," and at a
gathering of notables at Sokoto Lugard laid
down the first principles of the new *régime*.
On the one hand the British Government would
limit as far as possible the direct exercise of
its authority : it would not interfere with their

traditional system of monarchy, nor with their religion, nor with their Islamic law. On the other hand, it would use its power at need to prevent strife and disorder, and, above all else, it would forbid the continuance of the Slave Trade. By 1914, when the administration of all Nigeria was united under Sir Frederick Lugard as Governor-General, the life of its varied peoples had become as peaceful, orderly and prosperous as that of any " subject " people in the world. And the cats had been stopped from mousing.

The Brussels Act had only dealt with the Slave Trade, it had not raised the question of Slavery. But in British Tropical Africa, as in the West Indies or Mauritius, the complete extinction of the Trade by the occupation of its sources implied the extinction also, within measurable time, of the institution it had kept alive. The British Government did not accelerate the process as vigorously as some philanthropists in England would have wished. The difficulties of abrupt and enforced emancipation were an old West Indian story ; and it would not only have been far more unjust to impose it on a Moslem than on a Christian society without finding the vast sum needed to compensate the loss of property, it would have caused a far greater social upheaval and far greater distress to slaves as well as masters. The Government, therefore, decided to follow the precedent set by the Government of India in 1843. At an early stage in Nigeria and sooner or later in all the other occupied or " protected " territories the legal status of Slavery was abolished, the acquisition of new slaves prohibited, and every child born of slaves thereafter freed. In Sierra Leone, the oldest British colony in Africa, this method of " permissive emancipation " was not applied till 1928 when as many as 200,000 slaves were enabled, it is said, to assert their freedom. But if there or anywhere else beneath the British flag slaves still exist to-day because they do not choose to claim their rights, their number must be small, and before very long the last of them will have gone.

Thus by the time of the Great War the peoples of Europe, who in earlier days had taken so large a share in the enslavement of the peoples of Africa, had done something by way of atonement. Within the territories they controlled, they had destroyed the Slave Trade and well-nigh destroyed Slavery. And, if its almost inevitable entanglement in a world-wide conflict of Europe's making could be accounted as one more injury to Africa, it may be urged on the other side that among the immediate consequences of the war was a general revival of humanitarian ideals and their renewed application to Africa. Nowhere was this more apparent than in Article 22 of the Covenant of the League of Nations which, referring to the peoples of the territories conquered by the Allied Powers from the German and Turkish Empires, declared that "the well-being of such peoples form a sacred trust of civilization" and provided that the Powers to whom their "tutelage" was now to be committed should exercise it under the supervision of the League and in accordance with the terms of "Mandates" approved by the League. Among the stipulations of the Mandates applied to the ex-German colonies in Africa were the suppression of "all forms of Slave Trade" and "as speedy an elimination of domestic and other Slavery as social conditions will allow." In Tanganyika, accordingly, where the German Government had taken steps to ameliorate the conditions of Slavery and to facilitate manumission and had proclaimed the freedom of all children born from 1905 onwards, the further measure of abolishing the legal status of Slavery was at once adopted; and in the other two "mandated" territories assigned to Britain, parts of Togoland and of the Cameroons, the same result ensued from their administrative association with the Gold Coast and Nigeria.

This principle of "trusteeship" embodied in the Covenant was not new: the British Government, indeed, might claim that it had striven to apply it, sometimes, no doubt, with imperfect success, but sincerely and consistently since the days of Burke and Wilberforce. Nor could the principle be limited to the "mandated" territories: it obviously implied that all rule exercised by any of the Powers over any people

" not yet able to stand by themselves under the strenuous conditions of the modern world " was equally a " sacred trust." And it was in keeping with the atmosphere in which the Covenant was framed that the Allied Powers should resume at Paris the concerted efforts for the welfare of all Africa which had begun at Berlin and Brussels. Those earlier agreements had dealt only with the Slave Trade, but the Convention of St. Germain, signed in 1919, pledged its signatories " to endeavour to secure the complete suppression of Slavery in all its forms," including forced labour, pseudo-adoption, forced concubinage, and debt-slavery. That such further international effort was needed no one could doubt. Slavery, it is true, was dead or dying in practically all countries under European rule ; but slaves, whose total number reached into millions, were still to be found in other lands—in China, Arabia, Abyssinia and Liberia. To discover, as far as possible, the facts about this continuance of Slavery and to bring the pressure of world-opinion to bear on the Governments concerned with a view to its cessation, something more was needed than the limited Convention of St. Germain ; and in 1922 on the motion of Sir Arthur Steel-Maitland, acting as delegate of New Zealand, a resolution was adopted in the Assembly of the League putting the question of Slavery on its agenda and asking the Council to present a report thereon. In the following year the practical importance of the Slavery question was stressed by the terms of the admission of Abyssinia as a member of the League; in 1925 a Temporary Commission, on which Lord Lugard was the British representative, was appointed to investigate the subject; and in 1926 it presented a report recommending a new Anti-Slavery Convention to which not only the signatories of the Convention of St. Germain, nor only the members of the League, but all the States of the world should be invited to subscribe. The League accepted this proposal, and in 1926 a draft Convention, prepared by the British Government and presented by Lord Cecil, binding its signatories to bring about "progressively and as soon as possible the complete abolition of Slavery in all its forms," was approved and adopted and submitted to all Governments.

The publicity thus given to the question had its effect in more than one quarter. The British Government, under pressure in Parliament and from the Anti-Slavery Society, set itself to eliminate such remains of slavery as still lurked in corners of its scattered realm. The long overdue abolition of the legal status in Sierra Leone was enacted; and steps were taken to suppress the semi-servile custom of child-apprenticeship or ownership in Hong-Kong. Expeditions dispatched by the Governor of Burma penetrated into the remote and unexplored border-country of the province and obtained the release of all the slaves therein. Away on the north-eastern frontier of British India the Maharajah of Nepal, an independent State in old alliance with Britain, addressed to his people in 1924 a forcible and completely successful appeal that they should liberate their 50,000 slaves. In Abyssinia regulations were made to repress the Slave Trade and ameliorate Slavery, but they were ill-enforced ; the recalcitrant hillsmen of the frontier continued from time to time their slave-raids into adjacent British territory in the Sudan and Kenya ; and in 1931, the Emperor, Haile Sellassie, aware of world-opinion and determined to make a serious attempt to grapple with the peculiar difficulties of the problem in his country, invited the advice and assistance of the British Anti-Slavery Society. The invitation was accepted with the warm approval of the British Government ; a mission, headed by Lord Noel Buxton, great-grandson of the Emancipator, proceeded to Addis Ababa ; and after a full discussion with the Emperor and his ministers it came to the conclusion that Slavery might be actually abolished in Abyssinia in the course of fifteen or twenty years.

Thirty-eight States, meantime, had ratified the Convention of 1926 ; but it was felt in British circles that, despite the vast change in European sentiment since 1815, it would be difficult to make the Convention much more effective in practice than the Declaration of Vienna, unless some suitable machinery were devised to keep the question of Slavery to the fore and to facilitate its treatment. To this end a second Temporary Commission, appointed at the British Government's request, suggested the creation of an expert and authoritative international body charged with the permanent duty of watching the survivals of Slavery, reporting on measures taken to abolish it, and recommending to the League the best means of hastening the process : but the establishment of such a body was obstructed for a time by the fear lest it should encroach on the delicate ground of national sovereignty. In 1931, however, a vigorous move was made. On the motion of Earl Buxton, yet another member of the historic family, supported among others by Lord Lugard, the House of Lords declared its opinion that " the abolition of slave-owning, slave-trading, and slave-raiding is an urgent international duty . . . and that further steps of a definite nature appear to be required in order to bring about the extinction of Slavery in all its forms." The chief step in contemplation, as was clear from the debate, was the institution of a Permanent Slavery Commission, akin to the Mandates Commission, at Geneva ; and, with the Lords' resolution at its back, the British Government renewed its pressure to that end. This time it was successful. On October 12, 1932, the Assembly of the League adopted a resolution under which the Assembly of 1933 will be asked to vote the necessary funds for setting up an Advisory Committee of Experts, seven in number, appointed for an indefinite term to study, with the aid of a secretariat provided by the League, the primary problems of Slavery and to report at regular intervals to the Council. Thus the Convention is about to be supplied with the appropriate machinery for its execution, and there can be little doubt that, except perhaps in remote and unsettled regions of the world beyond the present reach of civilized opinion, the final eradication of the slave-system is assured in no long space of time.

The story thus concluded deals with only one aspect of a larger theme—the age-long contact between the diverse races of mankind, between white and coloured, between strong and weak ; and the knowledge of it should help the British people to do what they can to make that contact in the future a means of mutual understanding and co-operation rather than of conflict and oppression. For the story of the British anti-Slavery movement supplies the inspiration and incentive of a great popular tradition. It would be hard to overstate what the movement has owed to the character of its leaders—Sharp, Wilberforce, Clarkson, Macaulay, Buxton, Palmerston, Livingstone, Gordon, Kirk, Lugard and the rest— but they could not have done what they did if a great body of opinion among the British people had not been resolutely and persistently bent on the destruction of an evil which Britain had once done so much to create and sustain. There are dark and dubious passages enough in British history, but that one at least is clean—so clean that perhaps the praise accorded it by Lecky in his dry description of the rise and fall of moral forces in the European world is not much too high. "The unweary, unostentatious, and inglorious crusade of England against Slavery," he wrote, "may probably be regarded as among the three or four perfectly virtuous pages comprised in the history of nations."

7.4.34
Puerto Pollensa
Mallorca

NOTE ON BOOKS

Those who wish to pursue the subject of this volume further are recommended to read the following books, all of which are of relatively recent date.

(1) THE SLAVE-SYSTEM. W. L. Mathieson, *British Slavery and its Abolition, 1823–1838* (London, 1926, pp. 318), gives the best account of the slave-system in the West Indies. For the old American "South," see U. B. Phillips, *American Negro Slavery* (New York, 1918, pp. 529).

(2) THE EMANCIPATORS. E. C. P Lascelles, *Granville Sharp* (London, 1928, pp. 148). R. Coupland, *Wilberforce* (Oxford, 1923, pp. 517). C. Buxton, *Memoirs of Sir T. F. Buxton* (reprint, Everyman Series, London, pp. 264). The lives of Z. Macaulay by Viscountess Knutsford (London, 1900, pp. 489) and of Charles Grant by H. Morris (London, 1904, pp. 389) are out of print, but often obtainable second-hand. A life of Clarkson is expected shortly.

(3) THE ABOLITION OF THE BRITISH SLAVE TRADE AND SLAVERY. F. J. Klingberg, *The Anti-Slavery Movement in England* (New Haven and London, 1926), covers the period from 1770 to 1833. W. L. Mathieson, as cited in section (1) above, deals with the campaign of 1823–38 and describes the results in another book, *British Slave Emancipation, 1838–1849* (London, 1932, pp. 239). The biographies of the Emancipators in section (2) are largely concerned, of course, with Abolition.

(4) THE FOREIGN SLAVE TRADE. W. L. Mathieson, *Great Britain and the Slave Trade, 1839–65* (London, 1929, pp. 199), gives a full account of the British campaign. On American participation in the Trade and its suppression the standard work is W. E. B. Du Bois, *The Suppression of the African Slave Trade to the U.S.A.* (Cambridge, Mass., 1896, pp. 325); J. R. Spears, *The American Slave-Trade* (London, 1901, pp. 223), is more popular. T. Canot, *Memoirs of a Slave-Trader* (reprint, Travellers' Library, London, 1929, pp. 285), is interesting but probably unreliable in detail.

(5) THE ARAB SLAVE TRADE. References to this subject occur in most books about East Africa in the nineteenth century, but no full study of it has yet appeared. An account of it up to 1856 will be given in R. Coupland, *East Africa and its Invaders*, to be published in 1934. For the period 1858–73, the best information is in Livingstone's *Zambesi Expedition* and *Last Journals*, which are out of print, and in W. G. Blaikie, *Life of Livingstone* (popular reprint, London, 1925, pp. 397), R. J. Campbell, *Livingstone* (London, 1929, pp. 353), and R. Coupland, *Kirk on the Zambesi* (Oxford, 1928, pp. 278).

(6) THE LAST PHASE. Lord Lugard, *The Dual Mandate in British Tropical Africa*, (2nd ed., London, 1923, pp. 666); C. P. Lucas, *The Partition and Colonisation of Africa* (Oxford, 1922, pp. 218); H. H. Johnston, *The Opening-up of Africa* (Home University Library, pp. 254); I. Evans, *The British in Tropical Africa* (Cambridge, 1929, pp. 383); F. L. M. Moir, *After Livingstone* (London, pp. 200); B. M. Allen, *Gordon and the Sudan* (London, 1931, pp. 455). Details of the present-day Anti-Slavery Movement may be found in Lady Simon, *Slavery* (London, 1929, pp. 275); in Sir J. Harris, *A Century of Emancipation* (London, 1933); in current issues of the *Anti-Slavery Reporter*; and in official publications of the League of Nations. C. Lloyd. *Navy and the Slave Trade* (1949)

For further work on the subject such older books, now out of print, as Clarkson's *History of the Abolition of the Slave Trade*, J. Stephen's *Slavery of the British West India Colonies Delineated*, the long and detailed *Life of Wilberforce* by his sons, and Buxton's *African Slave Trade and its Remedy* will be needed. For these and other books, consult the bibliographies in Klingberg, as cited in section (3) above, and the *Cambridge History of the British Empire*, Vol. I, under "West Indies" and "West Africa."

INDEX

INDEX

254

INDEX

INDEX

Printed in Great Britain by Butler & Tanner Ltd., Frome and London

THE
HOME UNIVERSITY LIBRARY
OF MODERN KNOWLEDGE

Literature

† Also obtainable in Demy 8vo size, 7/6 net each.
*   „   „   „ Crown 8vo „ 5/- net each.

Political and Social Science

Religion and Philosophy

Science

A re-interpretation of the abolition
of the British Slave Trade
1806 – 1807.

= HR 1912
. . .

(Christian Vol 2. No 1.
Michaelmas 1955.
Reflexions on the History of
Christian Mission P. 69
R. Anster.
)